AF531751

# TEXTBOOK OF PROTISTOLOGY

# TEXTBOOK
# OF
# PROTISTOLOGY

Dr. D.R. Khanna
*Reader in Zoology*
*Gurukul Kangri University*
*Haridwar*
*(Uttaranchal)*
*(India)*

**DISCOVERY PUBLISHING HOUSE PVT. LTD.**
**NEW DELHI-110 002**

First Published - 2010

Reprinted - 2018

ISBN: 978-81-8356-570-7



**Textbook of Protistology**

*Published by:*

**DISCOVERY PUBLISHING HOUSE PVT. LTD.**

4383/4B, Ansari Road, Darya Ganj

New Delhi-110 002 (India)

*Phone*: +91-11-23279245, 43596064-65

*Fax*: +91-11-23253475

*E-mail*: discoverypublishinghouse@gmail.com

sales@discoverypublishinggroup.com

*web*: www.discoverypublishinggroup.com

*Printed at:*

Infinity Imaging Systems

Delhi

# Preface

Protists are a diverse group of eukaryotic microorganisms. Historically, protists were treated as the kingdom Protista but this group is no longer recognized in modern taxonomy. The protists do not have much in common besides a relatively simple organization—either they are unicellular, or they are multicellular wthout specialized tissues. This simple cellular organization distinguishes the protists from other eukaryotes, such as fungi, animals and plants.

The term 'protista' was first used by Ernst Haeckel in 1866. Protists were traditionally subdivided into several groups based on similarities to the "higher" kingdoms: the one-celled animal-like protozoa, the plant-like protophyta (mostly one-celled algae), and the fungus-like slime molds and water molds. Because these groups often overlap, they have been replaced by phylogenetic-based classifications. However, they are still useful as informal names for describing the morphology and ecology of protists.

Protists live in almost any environment that contains liquid water. Many protists, such as the algae, are photosynthetic and are vital primary producers in ecosystems, particularly in the ocean as part of the plankton. Other protists, such as the Kinetoplastids and Apicomplexa are responsible for a range of serious human diseases, such as malaria and sleeping sickness.

The first division of the protists from other organisms came in the 1820s, when the German biologist Georg A. Goldfuss introduced the word protozoa to refer to organisms such as ciliates and corals. This group was expanded in 1845 to include all "unicellular animals", such as Foraminifera and amoebae. The formal taxonomic category Protoctista was first proposed in the early 1860s John Hogg, who argued that the protists should include what he saw as primitive unicellular forms of both plants and animals. He defined the Protoctista as a "fourth kingdom of nature", in addition to the then-traditional kingdoms of plants, animals and minerals. The kingdom of minerals was later removed from taxonomy by Ernst Haeckel, leaving plants, animals, and the protists as a "kingdom of primitive forms".

**–Author**

# Contents

# Chapter–1

# Introduction

Protistology is a scientific discipline devoted to the study of protists. Its field of study overlaps with more traditional disciplines of algology, mycology, and protozoology, just as protists, which, being a paraphyletic group embrace algae, some organisms regarded previously as primitive fungi, and protozoa ("animal" motile protists lacking chloroplasts).

Protists are a diverse group of eukaryotic microorganisms. Historically, protists were treated as the kingdom Protista but this group is no longer recognized in modern taxonomy. The protists do not have much in common besides a relatively simple organisation—either they are unicellular, or they are multicellular wthout specialized tissues. This simple cellular organisation distinguishes the protists from other eukaryotes, such as fungi, animals and plants.

The term *protista* was first used by Ernst Haeckel in 1866. Protists were traditionally subdivided into several groups based on similarities to the "higher" kingdoms: the one-celled animal-like protozoa, the plant-like protophyta (mostly one-celled algae), and the fungus-like slime molds and water molds. Because these groups often overlap, they have been replaced by phylogenetic-based classifications. However, they are still useful as informal names for describing the morphology and ecology of protists.

Protists live in almost any environment that contains liquid water. Many protists, such as the algae, are photosynthetic and are vital primary producers in ecosystems, particularly in the ocean as part of the plankton. Other protists, such as the Kinetoplastids and Apicomplexa are responsible for a range of serious human diseases, such as malaria and sleeping sickness.

The first division of the protists from other organisms came in the 1820s, when the German biologist Georg A. Goldfuss introduced the word *protozoa* to refer to organisms such as ciliates and corals. This group was expanded in 1845 to include all "unicellular animals", such as Foraminifera and amoebae. The formal taxonomic category *Protoctista* was first proposed in the early 1860s by John Hogg, who argued that the protists should include what he saw as primitive unicellular forms of both plants and animals. He defined the Protoctista as a "fourth kingdom of nature", in addition to the then-traditional kingdoms of plants, animals and minerals. The kingdom of minerals was later removed from taxonomy by Ernst Haeckel, leaving plants, animals, and the protists as a "kingdom of primitive forms".

Herbert Copeland resurrected Hogg's label almost a century later, arguing that "Protoctista" literally meant "first established beings", Copeland complained that Haeckel's term *protista* included anucleated microbes such as bacteria. Copeland's use of the term *protoctista* did not. In contrast, Copeland's term included nucleated eukaryotes such as diatoms, green algae and fungi. This classification was the basis for Whittaker's later definition of Fungi, Animalia, Plantae and Protista as the four kingdoms of life The kingdom Protista was later modified to separate prokaryotes into the separate kingdom of Monera, leaving the protists as a group of eukaryotic microorganisms. These five kingdoms remained the accepted classification until the development of molecular phylogenetics in the late 20th century, when it became apparent that neither protists or monera were single groups of related organisms (they were not monophyletic groups).

**Modern Classifications**

Currently, the term *protist* is used to refer to unicellular eukaryotes that either exist as independent cells, or if they occur in colonies, do not show differentiation into tissues The term *protozoa* is used to refer to heterotrophic species of protists that do not form filaments. These terms are not used in current taxonomy, and are retained only as convenient ways to refer to these organisms.

The taxonomy of protists is still changing. Newer classifications attempt to present monophyletic groups based on ultrastructure, biochemistry, and genetics. Because the protists as a whole are paraphyletic, such systems often split up or abandon the kingdom, instead treating the protist groups as separate lines of eukaryotes.

Some of the main groups of protists, which may be treated as phyla, are listed in the taxobox at right. Many are thought to be monophyletic, though there is still uncertainty. For instance, the excavates are probably not monophyletic and the chromalveolates are probably only monophyletic if the haptophytes and cryptomonads are excluded.

## Types of Protists

### *Protozoa, the Animal-like Protists*

Protozoa are mostly single-celled, motile protists that feed by phagocytosis, though there are numerous exceptions. They are usually only 0.01–0.5 mm in size, generally too small to be seen without magnification. Protozoa are grouped by method of locomotion into:

| | |
|---|---|
| Flagellates | with long flagella e.g., *Euglena* |
| Amoeboids | with transient pseudopodia e.g., *Amoeba* |
| Ciliates | with multiple, short cilia e.g., *Paramecium* |
| Sporozoa | non-mobile parasites; some can form spores e.g., *Toxoplasma* |

### *Algae, the Plant-like Protists*

They include many single-celled organisms that are also considered protozoa, such as *Euglena*, which many believe have acquired chloroplasts through secondary endosymbiosis. Others are non-motile, and some (called seaweeds) are truly multicellular, including members of the following groups:

| | |
|---|---|
| Chlorophytes | green algae, are related to higher plants e.g., *Ulva* |
| Rhodophytes | red algae e.g., *Porphyra* |
| Heterokontophytes | brown algae, diatoms, etc. e.g., *Macrocystis* |

The green and red algae, along with a small group called the glaucophytes, appear to be close relatives of other plants, and so some authors treat them as Plantae despite their simple organisation. Most other types of algae, however, developed separately. They include the haptophytes, cryptomonads, dinoflagellates, euglenids, and chlorarachniophytes, all of which have also been considered protozoans.

Note some protozoa host endosymbiotic algae, as in *Paramecium bursaria* or radiolarians, that provide them with energy but are not integrated into the cell.

### *Fungus-like Protists*

Various organisms with a protist-level organisation were originally treated as fungi, because they produce sporangia. These include chytrids, slime molds, water molds, and Labyrinthulomycetes. Of these, the chytrids are now known to be related to other fungi and are usually classified with them. The others are now placed among the heterokonts (which have cellulose rather than chitin walls) and the Amoebozoa (which do not have cell walls).

## Metabolism

Protists obtain nutrients and digest nutrients in a complex acquirement and assimilation system. Many protists also feed on bacteria, these organisms engulf food and digest it internally. They extend their cell wall and cell membrane around the food material to form a food vacuole. This is then taken into the cell via endocytosis (usually phagocytosis; sometimes pinocytosis).

Nutrition in some different types of protists is variable. In flagellates, for example, filter feeding may sometimes occur where the flagella find the prey.

## Reproduction

Some protists reproduce sexually, while others reproduce asexually. Some species, for example *Plasmodium falciparum*, have extremely complex life cycles that involve multiple forms of the organism, some of which reproduce sexually and others asexually. However, it is unclear how frequently sexual reproduction causes genetic exchange between different strains of *Plasmodium* in nature and most populations of parasitic protists may be clonal lines that rarely exchange genes with other members of their species.

## Eukaryote

Animals, plants, fungi, and protists are **eukaryotes** organisms whose cells are organized into complex structures enclosed within membranes. The defining membrane-bound structure that differentiates eukaryotic cells from prokaryotic cells is the nucleus. The presence of a nucleus gives these organisms their name, which comes from the Greek (eu), meaning "good/ true," and (karyon), "nut." Many eukaryotic cells contain other membrane-bound organelles such as mitochondria, chloroplasts and Golgi bodies.

Cell division in eukaryotes is different from organisms without a nucleus (prokaryotes). It involves separating the duplicated chromosomes, through movements directed by microtubules. There are two types of division processes. In mitosis, one cell divides to produce two genetically-identical cells. In meiosis, which is required in sexual reproduction, one diploid cell (having two instances of each chromosome, one from each parent) undergoes recombination of each pair of parental chromosomes, and then two stages of cell division, resulting in four haploid cells (gametes). Each gamete has just one complement of chromosomes, each a unique mix of the corresponding pair of parental chromosomes.

Eukaryotes appear to be monophyletic, and so make up one of the three domains of life. The two other domains, bacteria and archaea, are prokaryotes, and have none of the above features. But eukaryotes do share some aspects of their biochemistry with archaea, and so are grouped with archaea in the clade Neomura.

## Cell Features

Eukaryotic cells are typically much larger than prokaryotes. They have a variety of internal membranes and structures, called organelles, and a cytoskeleton composed of microtubules, microfilaments, and intermediate filaments, which play an important role in defining the cell's organisation and shape. Eukaryotic DNA is divided into several linear bundles called chromosomes, which are separated by a microtubular spindle during nuclear division.

## Internal Membrane

Eukaryotic cells include a variety of membrane-bound structures, collectively referred to as the endomembrane system. Simple compartments, called vesicles or vacuoles, can form by budding off other membranes. Many cells ingest food and other materials through a process of endocytosis, where the outer membrane invaginates and then pinches off to form a vesicle. It is probable that most other membrane-bound organelles are ultimately derived from such vesicles.

The nucleus is surrounded by a double membrane (commonly referred to as a nuclear envelope), with pores that allow material to move in and out. Various tube- and sheet-like extensions of the nuclear membrane form what is called the endoplasmic reticulum or ER, which is involved in protein transport and maturation. It includes the rough ER where ribosomes are attached, and the proteins they synthesize enter the interior space or lumen. Subsequently, they generally enter vesicles, which bud off from the smooth ER. In most eukaryotes, these protein-carrying vesicles are released and further modified in stacks of flattened vesicles, called Golgi bodies or dictyosomes.

Vesicles may be specialized for various purposes. For instance, lysosomes contain enzymes that break down the contents of food vacuoles, and peroxisomes are used to break down peroxide, which is toxic otherwise. Many protozoa have contractile vacuoles, which collect and expel excess water, and extrusomes, which expel material used to deflect predators or capture prey. In multicellular organisms, hormones are often produced in vesicles. In higher plants, most of a cell's volume is taken up by a central vacuole, which primarily maintains its osmotic pressure.

**Mitochondria and Plastids**

Mitochondria are organelles found in nearly all eukaryotes. They are surrounded by double membranes (known as the phospholipid bi-layer), the inner of which is folded into invaginations called cristae, where aerobic respiration takes place. They contain their own DNA and ribosomes and are only formed by the fission of other mitochondria. They are now generally held to have developed from endosymbiotic prokaryotes, probably proteobacteria. The few protozoa that lack mitochondria have been found to contain mitochondrion-derived organelles, such as hydrogenosomes and mitosomes.

Plants and various groups of algae also have plastids. Again, these have their own DNA and developed from endosymbiotes, in this case cyanobacteria. They usually take the form of chloroplasts, which like cyanobacteria contain chlorophyll and produce energy through photosynthesis. Others are involved in storing food. Although plastids likely had a single origin, not all plastid-containing groups are closely related. Instead, some eukaryotes have obtained them from others through secondary endosymbiosis or ingestion.

Endosymbiotic origins have also been proposed for the nucleus, for which see below, and for eukaryotic flagella, supposed to have developed from spirochaetes. This is not generally accepted, both from a lack of cytological evidence and difficulty in reconciling this with cellular reproduction.

**Cytoskeletal Structures**

Many eukaryotes have long slender motile cytoplasmic projections, called flagella. These are composed mainly of tubulin and shorter cilia, both of which are variously involved in movement, feeding, and sensation. These are entirely distinct from prokaryotic flagella. They are supported by a bundle of microtubules arising from a basal body, also called a kinetosome or centriole, characteristically arranged as nine doublets surrounding two singlets. Flagella also may have hairs, or mastigonemes, and scales connecting membranes and internal rods. Their interior is continuous with the cell's cytoplasm. Microfilamental structures composed by actin and actin binding proteins, e.g., —actinin, fimbrin, filamin are present in submembraneous cortical layers and bundles, as well. Motor proteins of microtubules, e.g., dynein or kinesin and actin, e.g., myosins provide dynamic character of the network.

Centrioles are often present even in cells and groups that do not have flagella. They generally occur in groups of one or two, called kinetids, that give rise to various microtubular roots. These form a primary component of the cytoskeletal structure, and are often assembled over the course of several cell divisions, with one flagellum retained from the parent and the other derived from it. Centrioles may also be associated in the formation of a spindle during nuclear division.

Significance of cytoskeletal structures is underlined in determination of shape of the cells, as well as their being essential components of migratory responses like chemotaxis and chemokinesis. Some protists have various other microtubule-supported organelles. These include the radiolaria and heliozoa, which produce axopodia used in flotation or to capture prey, and the haptophytes, which have a peculiar flagellum-like organelle called the haptonema.

**Plant cell wall**

Plant cells have a cell wall, a fairly rigid layer outside the cell membrane, providing the cell with structural support, protection, and a filtering mechanism. The cell wall also prevents over-expansion when water enters the cell. The major carbohydrates making up the primary cell wall are cellulose, hemicellulose, and pectin. The cellulose microfibrils are linked via hemicellulosic tethers to form the cellulose-hemicellulose network, which is embedded in the pectin matrix. The most common hemicellulose in the primary cell wall is xyloglucan.

**Differences Between Eukaryotic Cells**

There are many different types of eukaryotic cells, though animals and plants are the most familiar eukaryotes, and thus provide an excellent starting point for understanding eukaryotic structure. Fungi and many protists have some substantial differences, however.

### Animal Cell

An animal cell is a form of eukaryotic cell that makes up many tissues in animals. The animal cell is distinct from other eukaryotes, most notably plant cells, as they lack cell walls and chloroplasts, and they have smaller vacuoles. Due to the lack of a rigid cell wall, animal cells can adopt a variety of shapes, and a phagocytic cell can even engulf other structures.

There are many different cell types. For instance, there are approximately 210 distinct cell types in the adult human body.

### Plant Cell

Plant cells are quite different from the cells of the other eukaryotic organisms. Their distinctive features are:

- A large central vacuole (enclosed by a membrane, the tonoplast), which maintains the cell's turgor and controls movement of molecules between the cytosol and sap;
- A primary cell wall containing cellulose, hemicellulose and pectin, deposited by the protoplast on the outside of the cell membrane; this contrasts with the cell walls of fungi, which contain chitin, and the cell envelopes of prokaryotes, in which peptidoglycans are the main structural molecules;
- The plasmodesmata, linking pores in the cell wall that allow each plant cell to communicate with other adjacent cells; this is different from the functionally analogous system of gap junctions between animal cells.
- Plastids, especially chloroplasts that contain chlorophyll, the pigment that gives plants their green colour and allows them to perform photosynthesis.
- Higher plants, including conifers and flowering plants (Angiospermae) lack the flagellae and centrioles that are present in animal cells.

## Fungal Cell

Fungal cells are most similar to animal cells, with the following exceptions:

- A cell wall containing chitin.
- Less definition between cells; the hyphae of higher fungi have porous partitions called septa, which allow the passage of cytoplasm, organelles, and, sometimes, nuclei. Primitive fungi have few or no septa, so each organism is essentially a giant multinucleate supercell; these fungi are described as coenocytic.
- Only the most primitive fungi, chytrids, have flagella.

## Other Eukaryotic Cells

Eukaryotes are a very diverse group, and their cell structures are equally diverse. Many have cell walls; many do not. Many have chloroplasts, derived from primary, secondary, or even tertiary endosymbiosis; and many do not. Some groups have unique structures, such as the cyanelles of the glaucophytes, the haptonema of the haptophytes, or the ejectisomes of the cryptomonads. Other structures, such as pseudopods, are found in various eukaryote groups in different forms, such as the lobose amoebozoans or the reticulose foraminiferans.

## Reproduction

Nuclear division is often coordinated with cell division. This generally takes place by mitosis, a process that allows each daughter nucleus to receive one copy of each chromosome. In most eukaryotes, there is also a process of sexual reproduction, typically involving an alternation between haploid generations, wherein only one copy of each chromosome is present, and diploid generations, wherein two are present, occurring through nuclear fusion (syngamy) and meiosis. There is considerable variation in this pattern, however.

Eukaryotes have a smaller surface to volume area ratio than prokaryotes, and thus have lower metabolic rates and longer generation times. In some multicellular organisms, cells specialized for metabolism will have enlarged surface areas, such as intestinal vili.

## Origin and Evolution

Phylogenetic tree showing the relationship between the eukaryotes and other forms of life. Eukaryotes are coloured red, archaea green and bacteria blue.

The origin of the eukaryotic cell was a milestone in the evolution of life, since they include all complex cells and almost all multi-cellular organisms. The timing of this series of events is hard to determine; Knoll (2006) suggests they developed approximately 1.6-2.1 billion years ago. Some acritarchs are known from at least 1650 million years ago, and the possible alga *Grypania* has been found as far back as 2100 million years ago. Fossils that are clearly related to modern groups start appearing around 1.2 billion years ago, in the form of a red alga.

Biomarkers suggest that at least stem eukaryotes arose even earlier. The presence of steranes in Australian shales indicates that eukaryotes were present 2.7 billion years ago.

rRNA trees constructed during the 1980s and 1990s left most eukaryotes in an unresolved "crown" group (not technically a true crown), which was usually divided by the form of the mitochondrial cristae; see crown eukaryotes. The few groups that lack mitochondria branched separately, and so the absence was believed to be primitive; but this is now considered an artifact of long-branch attraction, and they are known to have lost them secondarily.

Trees based on actin and other molecules have painted a different and more complete picture. Most eukaryotes are now included in one of the following supergroups, although the relationship between these groups, and the monophyly of each group, is not yet clear:

| | |
|---|---|
| Opisthokonts | Animals, fungi, choanoflagellates, etc. |
| Amoebozoa | Most lobose amoebae and slime moulds |
| Rhizaria | Foraminifera, Radiolaria, and various other amoeboid protozoa |
| Excavates | Various flagellate protozoa |

| | |
|---|---|
| Archaeplastida (or Primoplantae) | Land plants, green algae, red algae, and glaucophytes |
| Chromalveolates | Heterokonts, Haptophytes, Cryptomonads, and Alveolates. |

Several authorities recognize two larger clades, the unikonts and the bikonts, that derive from an ancestral uniflagellar organism and a biflagellate, respectively. In this system, the opisthokonts and amoebozoans are considered unikonts, and the rest bikonts. The chromalveolates were originally thought to be two separate groups, the chromists and the alveolates, but the former was proved to be paraphyletic to the latter, and the two groups combined. Some small protist groups have not been related to any of these supergroups, in particular the centrohelids.

Eukaryotes are closely related to Archaea, at least in terms of nuclear DNA and genetic machinery, and some place them with Archaea in the clade Neomura. In other respects, such as membrane composition, they are similar to eubacteria. Three main explanations for this have been proposed:

- Eukaryotes resulted from the complete fusion of two or more cells, wherein the cytoplasm formed from a eubacterium, and the nucleus from an archaeon, or from a virus.
- Eukaryotes developed from Archaea, and acquired their eubacterial characteristics from the proto-mitochondrion.
- Eukaryotes and Archaea developed separately from a modified eubacterium.

The origins of the endomembrane system and mitochondria are also unclear The phagotrophic hypothesis proposes that eukaryotic-type membranes lacking a cell wall originated first, with the development of endocytosis, whereas mitochondria were acquired by ingestion as endosymbionts. The syntrophic hypothesis proposes that the proto-eukaryote relied on the proto-mitochondrion for food, and so ultimately grew to surround it. Here the membranes originated after the engulfment of the mitochondrion, in part thanks to mitochondrial genes (the hydrogen hypothesis is one particular version).

In a study using genomes to construct supertrees, Pisani *et al* (2007) suggest that, along with evidence that there was never a mitochondrion-less eukaryote, eukaryotes evolved from a syntrophy between an archaea closely related to Thermoplasmatales and an a-proteobacterium, likely a symbiosis driven by sulfur or hydrogen. The mitochondrion and its genome is a remnant of the a-proteobacterial endosymbiont.

# Chapter–2

# Algae

## INTRODUCTION

Algae (*sing*. alga) are a large and diverse group of simple, typically autotrophic organisms, ranging from unicellular to multicellular forms.

There are nearly 30,000 algae species. The largest and most complex marine forms are called seaweeds, with 10,000 species. They are photosynthetic, like plants, and "simple" because they lack the many distinct organs found in land plants. Though the prokaryotic *cyanobacteria* (commonly referred to as blue-green algae) were traditionally included as "algae" in older textbooks, many modern sources regard this as outdated and restrict the term *algae* to eukaryotic organisms.

All true algae therefore have a nucleus enclosed within a membrane and chloroplasts bound in one or more membranes. Algae constitute a paraphyletic and polyphyletic group, as they do not all descend from a common algal ancestor, although their chloroplasts seem to have a single origin.

Algae lack the various structures that characterize land plants, such as phyllids and rhizoids in nonvascular plants, or leaves, roots, and other organs that are found in tracheophytes. They are distinguished from protozoa in that they are photosynthetic. Many are photoautotrophic, although some groups contain members that are mixotrophic, deriving energy both from photosynthesis and uptake of organic carbon either by osmotrophy, myzotrophy, or phagotrophy. Some unicellular species rely entirely on external energy sources and have limited or no photosynthetic apparatus.

All algae have photosynthetic machinery ultimately derived from the cyanobacteria, and so produce oxygen as a by-product of photosynthesis, unlike other photosynthetic bacteria such as purple and green sulfur bacteria.

## Ecology

Algae are most prominent in bodies of water, but are also common in terrestrial environments. However, terrestrial algae are usually rather inconspicuous and far more common in moist, tropical regions than dry ones, because algae lack vascular tissues and other adaptations to live on land. Algae are also found in other situations, such as on snow and on exposed rocks in symbiosis with a fungus as lichen.

The various sorts of algae play significant roles in aquatic ecology. Microscopic forms that live suspended in the water column (phytoplankton) provide the food base for most marine food chains. In very high densities (so-called algal blooms) these algae may discolour the water and outcompete, poison, or asphyxiate other life forms. Seaweeds grow mostly in shallow marine waters, however some have been recorded to a depth of 300 m ome are used as human food or harvested for useful substances such as agar, carrageenan, or fertilizer.

## Study of Algae

The study of marine and freshwater algae is called phycology or algology. The US Algal Collection is represented by almost 300,000 accessioned and inventoried herbarium specimens.

## Classification

While *Cyanobacteria* have been traditionally included among the algae, referred to as the Cyanophytes or blue-green algae, recent works on algae usually exclude them due to large differences such as the lack of membrane-bound organelles, the presence of a single circular chromosome, the presence of peptidoglycan in the cell walls, and ribosomes different in size and content from eukaryotes . Rather than in chloroplasts, they conduct photosynthesis on specialized infolded cytoplasmic membranes called thylakoid membranes. Therefore, they differ significantly from the algae despite occupying similar ecological niches.

By modern definitions algae are eukaryotes and conduct photosynthesis within membrane-bound organelles called chloroplasts. Chloroplasts contain circular DNA and are similar in structure to cyanobacteria, presumably representing reduced cyanobacterial endosymbionts. The exact nature of the chloroplasts is different among the different lines of algae, reflecting different endosymbiotic events. The table below lists the three major groups of algae and their lineage relationship is shown in the figure on the left. Note many of these groups contain some members that are no longer photosynthetic. Some retain plastids, but not chloroplasts, while others have lost them entirely.

These algae have *primary* chloroplasts, i.e. the chloroplasts are surrounded by *two membranes* and probably developed through a single endosymbiotic event. The chloroplasts of red algae have chlorophylls *a* and *d* (often), and phycobilins, while those of the green alga have chloroplasts with chlorophyll *a* and *b*. Higher plants are pigmented similarly to green algae and probably developed from them, and thus Chlorophyta is a sister taxon to the plants; sometimes they are grouped as Viridiplantae.

These groups have green chloroplasts containing chlorophylls *a* and *b*. Their chloroplasts are surrounded by *four and three membranes*, respectively, and were probably retained from an ingested green alga.

Chlorarachniophytes, which belong to the phylum Cercozoa, contain a small nucleomorph, which is a relict of the alga's nucleus.

Euglenids, which belong to the phylum Euglenozoa, live primarily in freshwater and have chloroplasts with only three membranes. It has been suggested that the endosymbiotic green algae were acquired through myzocytosis rather than phagocytosis.

These groups have chloroplasts containing chlorophylls *a* and *c*, and phycobilins. The latter chlorophyll type is not known from any prokaryotes or primary chloroplasts, but genetic similarities with the red algae suggest a relationship there.

In the first three of these groups (Chromista), the chloroplast has four membranes, retaining a nucleomorph in cryptomonads, and they likely share a common pigmented ancestor, although other evidence casts doubt on whether the Heterokonts, Haptophyta, and Cryptomonads are in fact more closely related to each other than other groups.

The typical dinoflagellate chloroplast has three membranes, but there is considerable diversity in chloroplasts among the group, and it appears there were a number of endosymbiotic events here. The Apicomplexa, a group of closely related parasites, also have plastids called apicoplasts. Apicoplasts are not photosynthetic but appear to have a common origin with dinoflagellates chloroplasts.

## FORMS OF ALGAE

Most of the simpler algae are unicellular flagellates or amoeboids, but colonial and non-motile forms have developed independently among several of the groups. Some of the more common organisational levels, more than one of which may occur in the life cycle of a species, are

- *Colonial*: small, regular groups of motile cells
- *Capsoid*: individual non-motile cells embedded in mucilage
- *Coccoid*: individual non-motile cells with cell walls
- *Palmelloid*: non-motile cells embedded in mucilage
- *Filamentous*: a string of non-motile cells connected together, sometimes branching.
- *Parenchymatous*: cells forming a thallus with partial differentiation of tissues.

In three lines even higher levels of organisation have been reached, with full tissue differentiation. These are the brown algae, some of which may reach 50 m in length (kelps) the red algae, and the green algae. The most complex forms are found among the green algae, in a lineage that eventually led to the higher land plants. The point where these non-algal plants begin and algae stop is usually taken to be the presence of reproductive organs with protective cell layers, a characteristic not found in the other alga groups.

The first plants on earth evolved from shallow freshwater algae much like *Chara* some 400 million years ago. These probably had an isomorphic alternation of generations and were probably heterotrichous. Fossils of isolated land plant spores suggest land plants may have been around as long as 475 million years ago.

**Algae and Symbioses**

Some species of algae form symbiotic relationships with other organisms. In these symbioses, the algae supply photosynthates (organic substances) to the host organism providing protection to the algal cells. The host organism derives some or all of its energy requirements from the algae. Examples include:

- *lichens*: a fungus is the host, usually with a green alga or a cyanobacterium as its symbiont. Both fungal and algal species found in lichens are capable of living independently, although habitat requirements may be greatly different from those of the lichen pair.
- *corals*: algae known as zooxanthellae are symbionts with corals. Notable amongst these is the dinoflagellate *Symbiodinium*, found in many hard corals. The loss of *Symbiodinium*, or other zooxanthellae, from the host is known as coral bleaching.
- *sponges*: green algae live close to the surface of some sponges, for example, breadcrumb sponge (*Halichondria panicea*). The alga is thus protected from predators; the sponge is provided with oxygen and sugars which can account for 50 to 80% of sponge growth in some species.

**Life-cycle**

Rhodophyta, Chlorophyta and Heterokontophyta, the three main algal Phyla, have life-cycles which show tremendous variation with considerable complexity. In general there is an asexual phase where the seaweed's cells are diploid, a sexual phase where the cells are haploid followed by fusion of the male and female gametes. Asexual reproduction is advantageous in that it permits efficient population increases, but less variation is possible. Sexual reproduction allows more variation but is more costly because of the waste of gametes that fail to mate, among other things. Often there is no strict alternation between the sporophyte and gametophyte phases and also because there is often an asexual phase, which could include the fragmentation of the thallus.

## NUMBERS AND DISTRIBUTION

In the British Isles the UK Biodiversity Steering Group Report estimated there to be 20,000 algal species in the UK, freshwater and marine, about 650 of these are seaweeds. Another checklist of freshwater algae reported only about 5000 species. It seems therefore that the 20,000 is an overestimate or an error. The Smithsonian collection of algae has over 300,000 specimens. Worldwide it is thought that there are over 5,000 species of red algae, 1,500 — 2,000 of brown algae and 8,000 of green algae. In Australia it is estimated that there are over 1,300 species of red algae, 350 species of brown algae and approximately 2,000 species of green algae totalling 3,650 species of algae in Australia. Around 400 species appear to be an average figure for the coastline of South African west coast. 669 marine species have been described from California (U.S.A.). 642 entities are listed in the check-list of Britain and Ireland.

## USES OF ALGAE

### Fertilizer

For centuries seaweed has been used as a fertilizer; Orwell writing in the 16th century referring to drift weed in South Wales: "This kind of ore they often gather and lay in heaps where it heats and rots, and will have a strong and loathsome smell; when being so rotten they cast it on the land, as they do their muck, and thereof springeth good corn, especially barley" and "After spring tides or great rigs of the sea, they fetch it in sacks on horse brackets, and carry the same three, four, or five miles, and cast it on the lande, which doth very much better the ground for corn and grass".

Algae are used by humans in many ways. They are used as fertilizers, soil conditioners and are a source of livestock feed Because many species are aquatic and microscopic, they are cultured in clear tanks or ponds and either harvested or used to treat effluents pumped through the ponds. Algaculture on a large scale is an important type of aquaculture in some places.

Maerl is commonly used as a soil conditioner, it is dredged from the sea floor and crushed to form a powder. It is still harvested around the coasts of Brittany in France and off Falmouth, Cornwall (also extensively in western Ireland) and is a popular fertilizer in these days of organic gardening investigated Falmouth maerl and found that *L. corallioides* predominated down to 6 m and *P. calcareum* from 6-10 m.

**Energy Source**

- Algae can be grown to produce biohydrogen. In 1939 a German researcher named. Hans Gaffron, while working at the University of Chicago, observed that the algae he was studying, *Chlamydomonas reinhardtii* (a green-alga), would sometimes switch from the production of oxygen to the production of hydrogen. Gaffron never discovered the cause for this change and for many years other scientists failed to repeat his findings. In the late 1990s professor Anastasios Melis, a researcher at the University of California at Berkeley, discovered that if the algae culture medium is deprived of sulfur it will switch from the production of oxygen (normal photosynthesis), to the production of hydrogen. He found that the enzyme responsible for this reaction is hydrogenase, but that the hydrogenase lost this function in the presence of oxygen. Melis found that depleting the amount of sulfur available to the algae interrupted its internal oxygen flow, allowing the hydrogenase an environment in which it can react, causing the algae to produce hydrogen. *Chlamydomonas moeweesi* is also a good strain for the production of hydrogen. Scientists at the U.S. Department of Energy's Argonne National Laboratory are currently trying to find a way to take the part of the hydrogenase enzyme that creates the hydrogen gas and introduce it into the photosynthesis process. The result would be a large amount of hydrogen gas, possibly on par with the amount of oxygen created.

- Algae can be used to make biodiesel (see algaculture), bioethanol and biobutanol and by some estimates can produce vastly superior amounts of vegetable oil, compared to terrestrial crops grown for the same purpose.
- Algae can be used in oil production which could replace the petrol and other gas products in the near future.
- Algae can be grown to produce biomass, which can be burned to produce heat and electricity.

**Pollution Control**

- Algae are used in wastewater treatment facilities, reducing the need for greater amounts of toxic chemicals than are already used.
- Algae can be used to capture fertilizers in runoff from farms. When subsequently harvested, the enriched algae itself can be used as fertilizer.
- Algae Bioreactors are used by some powerplants to reduce $CO_2$ emissions. The $CO_2$ can be pumped into a pond, or some kind of tank, on which the algae feed. Alternatively, the bioreactor can be installed directly on top of a smokestack. This technology has been pioneered by Massachusetts-based Green Fuel Technologies.

**Stabilizing Substances**

*Chondrus crispus* (probably confused with *Mastocarpus stellatus*, common name: Irish moss), is also used as "carrageen". The name carrageenan comes from the Irish Gaelic for *Chondrus crispus*. It is an excellent stabiliser in milk products - it reacts with the milk protein caesin, other products include: petfoods, toothpaste, ice-creams and lotions etc. Alginates in creams and lotions are absorbable through the skin.

## Nutrition

Seaweeds are an important source of food, especially in Asia; They are excellent sources of many vitamins including: A, B1, B2, B6, niacin and C. They are rich in iodine, potassium, iron, magnesium and calcium.

Algae is commercially cultivated as a nutritional supplement. One of the most popular microalgal species is Spirulina *(Arthrospira platensis)*, which is a Cyanobacteria (known aş blue-green algae), and has been hailed by some as a superfood. Other algal species cultivated for their nutritional value include; Chlorella (a green algae), and Dunaliella (*Dunaliella salina*), which is high in beta-carotene and is used in vitamin C supplements.

In China at least 70 species of algae are eaten as is the Chinese "vegetable" known as *fat choy* (which is actually a cyanobacterium). Roughly 20 species of algae are used in everyday cooking in Japan.

Certain species are edible; the best known, especially in Ireland is *Palmaria palmata* (Linnaeus) O. Kuntze, also known as *Rhodymenia palmata* (Linnaeus) Kuntze, common name: dulse). is is a red alga which is dried and may be bought in the shops in Ireland. It is eaten raw, fresh or dried, or cooked like spinach. Similarly, *Durvillaea antarctica* is eaten in Chile, common name: cochayuyo.

*Porphyra* (common name: purple laver), is also collected and used in a variety of ways (e.g. "laver bread" in the British Isles). In Ireland it is collected and made into a jelly by stewing or boiling. Preparation also involves frying with fat or converting to a pinkish jelly by heating the fronds in a saucepan with a little water and beating with a fork. It is also collected and used by people parts of Asia, specifically China, Korea (gim) and Japan (nori) and along most of the coast from California to British Columbia. The Hawaiians and the Maoris of New Zealand also use it.

One particular use is in "instant" puddings, sauces and creams. *Ulva lactuca* (common name: sea lettuce), is used locally in Scotland where it is added to soups or used in salads. *Alaria esculenta* (common name: badderlocks or dabberlocks), is used either fresh or cooked, in Greenland, Iceland, Scotland and Ireland.

The oil from some algae have high levels of unsaturated fatty acids. Arachidonic acid (a polyunsaturated fatty acid), is very high in *Parietochloris incisa,* (a green alga) where it reaches up to 47% of the triglyceride pool.

Some varieties of algae are a vegetarian/vegan/plant based source of long chain essential omega-3 fatty acids Docosahexaenoic acid (DHA) and Eicosapentaenoic acid (EPA) in addition to vitamin B12. Fish oil contains the omega-3 fatty acids, but the original source is algae, which are eaten by marine life such as copepods and passed up the food chain.

**Other Uses**

There are also commercial uses of algae as agar. The natural pigments produced by algae can be used as an alternative to chemical dyes and colouring agents. Many of the paper products used today are not recyclable because of the chemical inks that they use, paper recyclers have found that inks made from algae are much easier to break down. There is also much interest in the food industry into replacing the colouring agents that are currently used with colouring derived from algal pigments. Algae can be used to make pharmaceuticals Sewage can be treated with algae as well Some cosmetics can come from microalgae as well. In Israel, a species of green algae is grown in water tanks, then exposed to direct sunlight and heat which causes it to become bright red in colour. It is then harvested and used as a natural pigment for foods such as Salmon.

**Alginates**

Between 100,000 and 170,000 wet tons of *Macrocystis* are harvested annually in California for alginate extraction and abalone feed.

**Collecting and Preserving Specimens**

Seaweed specimens can be collected and preserved for research. Such preserved specimens will keep for two or three hundred years. Those of Carl von Linné (1707-1778) are still available for reference, and are used. Specimens may be collected from the shore; those below low tide must be collected by diving or dredging. The whole algal specimen should be collected, that is the holdfast, stipe and lamina. Specimens of algae reproducing will be the more useful for identification and research. When collected the details of the location and site should be noted. They can then be preserved pressed on paper or in a preserving liquid such as alcohol or solution of 5 per cent formalin/seawater. However, formalin is reported to be carcinogenic.

## Ecology

### *Biological Exposure Scale*

The ecology of the shores of the British Isles, including a discussion of the different shores from sheltered to exposed along with an exposure scale. An exposure scale of five stages is given:- Very Exposed Shores; Exposed Shores; Semi-exposed Shores; Sheltered Shores and Very Sheltered Shores.

Factors indicating the differences between these exposure scales are detailed. Very Exposed Shores have a wide *Verrucaria* zone entirely above the upper tide level, a *Porphyra* zone above the barnacle level and *Lichina pygmaea* is locally abundant. The eulittoral zone is dominated by barnacles and limpets with a coralline belt in the very low littoral along with other Rhodophyta and *Alaria* in the upper sublittoral. Exposed shores show a *Verrucaria* belt mainly above the high tide, with *Porphyra* and *Lichina pygmaea*. The mid-shore is dominated by barnacles, limpets and some *Fucus*. Some Rhodophyta. *Himanthalia* and some Rhodophyta such as *Mastocarpus* and *Corallina* are found in the low littorral with *Himanthalia, Alaria* and *Laminaria digitata* dominant in the upper sublittoral. The semi-exposed shores show a *Verrucaria* belt just above high tide with clear *Pelvetia* in the upper-littoral and *Fucus serratus* in the lower-littoral. Limpets, barnacles and short *Fucus vesiculosus* midshore. *Fucus serratus* with Rhodophyta, (*Laurencia, Mastocarpus stellatus, Rhodymenia* and *Lomentaria*). *Laminaria* and *Saccorhiza polyschides* and small algae common in the sublittoral. The sheltered shores show a narrow *Verrucaria* zone at high water and a full sequence of fucoids: *Pelvetia, Fucus spiralis, Fucus vesiculosus, Fucus serratus, Ascophyllum nodosum*. *Laminaria digitata* is dominant the upper sublittoral. The very sheltered shores show a very narrow zone of *Verrucaria*, the dominance of the littoral by a full sequence of the fucoids and *Ascophyllum* covering the rocks. *Laminaria saccharina, Halidrys, Chondrus* and or *Furcellaria*.

**Common Names of Algae**

- *Alaria sculenta* Dabberlocks; Edible kelp
- *Ascophyllum nodosum* Knotted wrack
- *Chondrus crispus* Carragheen; Irish moss
- *Chorda filum* Sea lace
- *Colpomena peregrina* Oyster thief
- *Fucus* Wrack
- *Fucus ceranoides* Horned wrack
- *Fucus serratus* Toothwrack
- *Fucus vesiculosus* Bladderwrack
- *Fucus spirals* Spiral wrack
- *Himanthalia elongata* Sea thong Thong-weed
- *Laminaria digitata* Tangle Oarweed
- *Laminaria hyperborea* Curvie
- *Laminaria saccharina* Sea belt; Sugar Kelp; Sugarwrack
- *Laurencia pinnatifida* Pepper dulse
- *Padin pavonia* Peacocks
- *Palmaria palmata* Dulse
- *Pelvetia canaliculata* Channelled wrack
- *Plocamium vulgare* Cockscomb
- *Polyides caprinus* Goat tang
- *Polysiphonia elongata* Lobster horns

- *Porphyra umbilicalis* Purple laver; Laver
- *Saccorhiza polyschides* Furbelows
- *Ulva lactuca* Sea lettuce

**Examples**

- *Atractophora hypnoides* P.L.Crouan and H.M.Crouan (red algae)
- *Ascophyllum nodosum*
- *Charales* (green algae)
- *Codium*
- *Fucus*
- *Ulva lactuca*
- *Laminaria*
- *Lemanea*
- *Macrocystis*
- *Mastocarpus stellatus*
- *Pelvetia canaliculata*
- *Palmaria palmata*
- *Porphyra*
- *Postelsia palmaeformis*

## Chapter–3

# Eukaryotes and Protists

### INTRODUCTION

The transition to eukaryotic cells appears to have occurred during the Proterozoic Era, about 1.2 to 1.5 billion years ago. However, recent genetic studies suggest eukaryotes diverged from prokaryotes closer to 2 billion years ago. Fossils do not yet agree with this date. The old Kingdom Protista, thus contains some living groups that might serve as possible models for the early eukaryotes. This taxonomic kingdom has been broken into many new kingdoms, reflecting new studies and techniques that help elucidate the true phylogenetic sequence of life on Earth.

Protists exhibit a great deal of variation in their life histories (life cycles). They exhibit an alternation between diploid and haploid phases (Fig. 3.1) that is similar to the alternation of generations found in plants. Protist life cycles vary from diploid dominant, to haploid dominant.

The great diversity of form, habitat, mode of nutrition, and life history exhibited by eukaryotes suggests they evolved several times from various groups of prokaryotes. This makes the Protista a polyphyletic group. Eukaryotes are generally larger, have a variety of membrane-bound organelles, greater internal complexity than prokaryotic cells, and has a secialized method of cell division (meiosis) that is a prelude to true sexual reproduction. Protists might be viewed as a group from which the other eukaryotic kingdoms evolved.

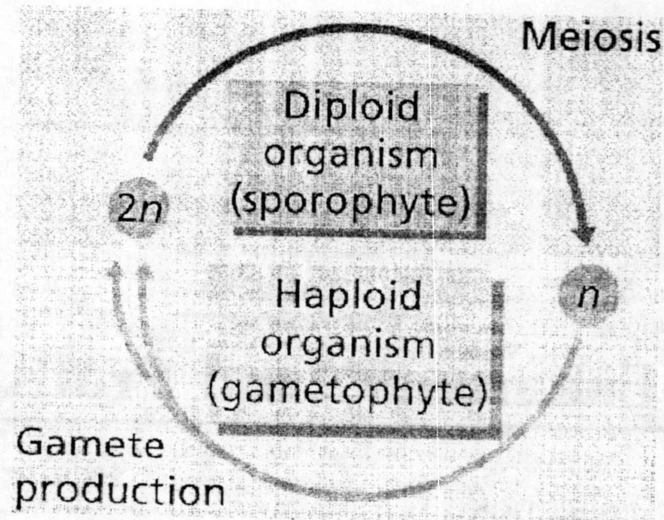


*Fig. 3.1*

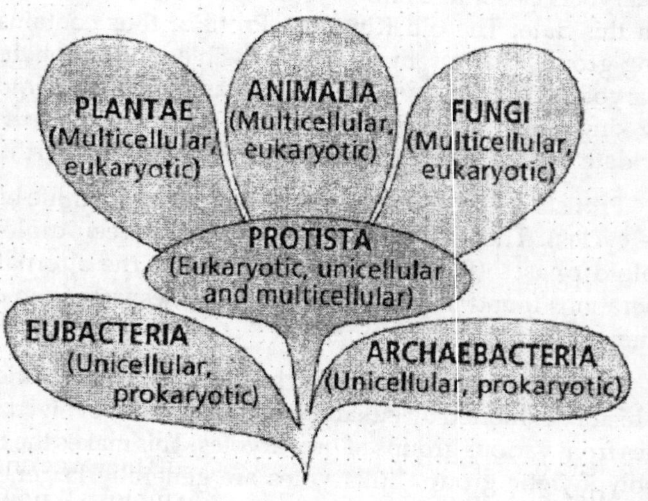


***Fig. 3.2*: The "six" kingdom taxonomic scheme**

## Eukaryotic Organelles and Prokaryotic Symbionts

Symbiosis is the interactive association of two or more species living together. There are several types of symbiosis. Parasitism is a symbiosis where one organism causes harm to the other, its host. An example of this is a disease causing bacterium, such as *Treponema pallidum*, which causes the disease syphilis in humans. Commensalism is a symbiosis where one organism benefits and the other is not harmed or helped. The symbiotic relationship between alge and fungi in lichens is an example of this. Mutualism is a symbiosis where both organisms benefit. Mutualism examples are abundant: zooxanthellae are dinoflagellates that live within the body of coral; *E. coli* bacteria live in the human intestine; etc.

The symbiotic model proposed by American biologist Lynn Margulis suggests possible symbiosis of bacteria within early eukaryotic cells (Fig. 3.3). Margulis proposed the mechanism of endosymbiosis, to explain the origin of mitochondria and chloroplasts from permanent resident prokaryotes. According to this idea, a larger prokaryote (or perhaps early eukaryote) engulfed or surrounded a smaller prokaryote some 1.5 billion to 700 million years ago.

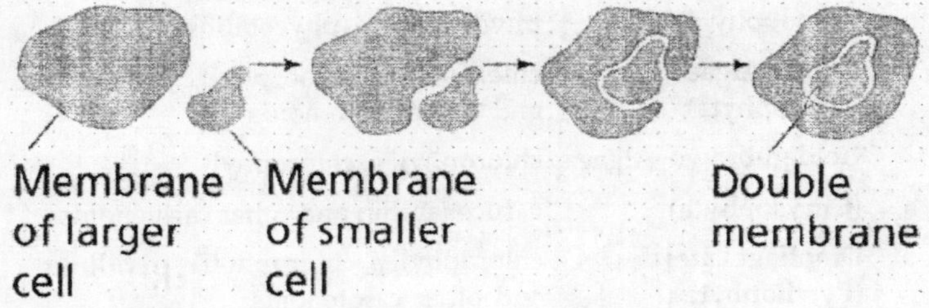


*Fig. 3.3*

Instead of digesting the smaller organisms the large one and the smaller one entered into a type of symbiosis known as mutualism, where both organisms benefit and neither is harmed. The larger organism gained excess ATP provided by the "protomitochondrion" and excess sugar provided by the "protochloroplast", while providing a stable environment and the raw materials the endosymbionts required. This has become so strong a symbiosis that eukaryotic cells cannot survive without their mitochondria (likewise photosynthetic eukaryotes cannot survive without their chloroplasts), and the endosymbionts cannot survive outside their hosts. Nearly all (but not ALL) eukaryotes have mitochondria. Mitochondrial division is remarkably similar to the prokaryotic methods that were studied in the cell division and bacterial diversity chapters.

Chloroplasts and mitochondria still retain their own DNA, and have the diversity of structure and photosynthetic pigments that supports the idea that the endosymbiosis events occurred independantly several times. The photosynthetic pigments (Table 3.1) in the red, brown, golden-brown, and green algae are very different, lending support for the hypothesis of several different, independent endosymbiotic events.

**Table 3.1**

| | |
|---|---|
| Cyanobacteria | chlorophyll *a*, chlorophyll *c*, phycocyanin, phycoerythrin |
| Chloroxybacteria | chlorophyll *a*, chlorophyll *b* |
| Green Algae (Chlorophyta) | chlorophyll *a*, chlorophyll *b*, carotenoids |
| Red Algae (Rhodophyta) | chlorophyll *a*, phycocyanin, phycoerythrin, phycobilins |
| Brown Algae (Phaeophyta) | chlorophyll *a*, chloorphyll c, fucoxanthin and other carotenoids |
| Golden-brown Algae (Chrysophyta) | chlorophyll *a*, chlorophyll c, fucoxanthin and other carotenoids |
| Dinoflagellates (Pyrrhophyta) | chlorophyll *a*, chlorophyll *c*, peridinin and other carotenoids |
| Vascular Plants | chlorophyll *a*, chlorophyll *b*, carotenoids |

The DNA, ribosomes, biochemistry, and reproduction of chloroplasts and mitochondria are remarkably bacteria-like. Some living eukaryotes, such as the "amoeba" *Pelomyxa* (also known as *Chaos*), lack mitochondria, having instead endosymbiotic bacteria that perform mitochondrial duties of ATP generation.

## CLASSIFICATION OF PROTISTS

The protists include heterotrophs, autotrophs, and some organisms that can vary their nutritional mode depending on environmental conditions. Protists occur in freshwater, saltwater, soil, and as symbionts within other organisms. Due to this tremendous diversity, classification of the Protista is difficult.

Historically the group has been subdivied based on the mode of nutrition, photosynthestic pigments, and the type of organelles used for locomotion. For example, the organisms using cilia to propel themselves were all placed in the Phylum Ciliata; those using pseudopodia were all in the Phylum Sarcodina. This is an example of form classification, and worked well enough until scientists began to examine the protists both biochemically and ultratsructurally (with electron microscopes). They discovered the form classification mentioned above did not support the existence of monophyletic groups, and thus should be abandoned. Several new kingdoms have been proposed for the old protista, although consensus amongst systematists working with these groups has yet to fully emerge. Several organisms once placed in the protists have been moved to other Kingdoms, while others have moved from the Kingdom Fungi to the protists.

## KINGDOM ARCHAEZOA

Organisms placed in this proposed kingdom lack mitochondria. Scientists interpret this as an indication of the divergence of this group from other "protists" prior to the endosymbiosis event that led to the development of the mitochondrion. However, some recent studies seem to indicate that some of the organisms placed in this group are secondarily mitochondrialess: their ancestors had mitochondria but lost them over time. This casts doubt on the monophyletic nature of this proposed kingdom.

Members of the diplomonad subgroup of archaezoans have two flagella, two nuclei, and no mitochondria. *Giardia lamblia,* an intestinal parasite that causes giardiasis, is a member of this group. A colourized scanning electron migrograph of this organism

## KINGDOM EUGLENOZOA

This proposed kingdom includes protists with one or two flagella emerging from an anterior pocket, and paramylum (a glucose polymer) as the storage product for sugars. Some members of this group are are autotrophic, while others are heterotrophic.

### Phylum Euglenophyta

Organisms in the Euglenophyta have two flagella, a contractile vacuole, a photoreceptive eyespot, several chloroplasts, lack a cell wall, and can live as either autotrophs or heterotrophs. Some autotrophic species of *Euglena*, become heterotrophic when light levels are low. Their chloroplasts are surrounded by three rather than the more typical two membranes. Euglenoid chloroplasts resemble those of green algae, and are probably derived from the green algae through endosymbiosis. However, the euglenoid pyrenoid produces an unusual type of carbohydrate polymer (paramylum) not seen in green algae.

Euglenoids lack cell walls. In its place, however, is a flexible pellicle composed of protein strips side. Euglenoids also have a contractile vacuole, like many other protists, for eliminating excess water. Euglenoids reproduce by longitudinal cell division, and sexual reproduction is not known to occur.

### Phylum Kinetoplastida

The other group within the Euglenozoa is the kinetoplastids. All members of this group are symbiotic, with some being parasitic. *Trypanosoma* is a kinetoplastid. *Trypanosoma brucei* is a trypanosome transmitted by the bite of the tsetse fly; it is the cause of African sleeping sickness.

### Kingdom Alveolata

The kingdom Alveolata was only recently recognized. The synapomorphy of this clade is the presence of small saccules (alveoli) below the cell membrane surface. Major groups in this kingdom are the ciliates, dinoflagellates and apicomplexans (a group of parasites that cause malaria and other diseases).

## Phylum Ciliophora

The phylum Ciliophora contains about 8,000 species of ciliates. Ciliates move by coordinated strokes of hundreds of cilia projecting through tiny holes in a semirigid pellicle. They discharge long, barbed trichocysts for defense and for capturing prey; toxicysts release a poison.

Ciliates are complex, heterotrophic protozoans that lack cell walls and use multiple small cilia for locomotion. To increase strength of the cell boundary, ciliates have a pellicle, a sort of tougher membrane that still allows them to change shape. Most of the 8000 species are freshwater. Most ciliates have two nuclei: a macronucleus that contains hundreds of copies of the genome and controls metabolisms, and a single small micronucleus that contains a single copy of the genome and functions in sexual reproduction. *Paramecium* is a common ciliate seen by students in introductory biology classes.

Since ciliates (an many freshwater protozoans) are hypotonic, removal of water crossing the cell membrane by osmosis is a significant problem. One commonly employed mechanism is a contractile vacuole (Fig. 3.4). Water is collected into the central ring of the vacuole and actively transported from the cell.

Food is taken into the cell by an oral groove, where small particles of the food are phagocytosed into food vacuoles. Often this can be accomplished in the laboratory period by using yeast stained with congo red dye, allowing students to see food vacuoles forming. The food vacuoles travel through the cytoplasm and are digested, with the molecules eventually passing into the cytoplasm, and wastes being expelled from the cell by exocytosis.

Ciliates travel along a spiral path with the cell rotating along its long axis and the direction of travel resembling a sine wave.

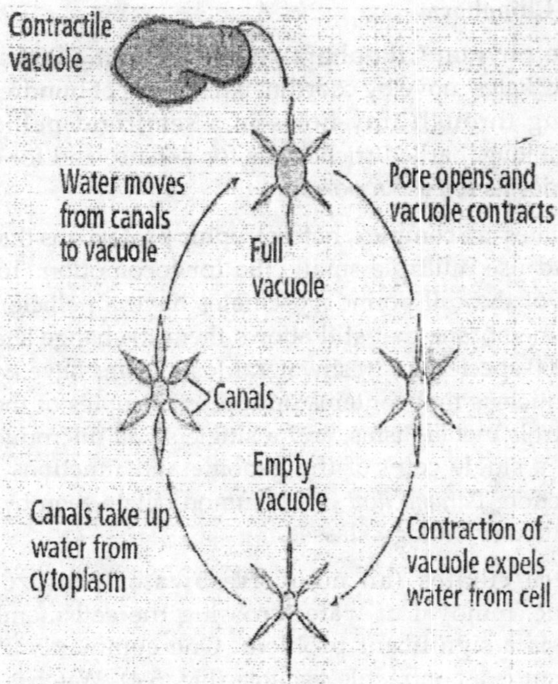


*Fig. 3.4:* **Functioning of a contractile vacuole in *Paramecium***

During asexual reproduction, ciliates divide by transverse binary fission. You may recall that bacteria have a somewhat similar type of binary fission, although no nuclei occur in bacteria.

Ciliates possess two types of nuclei—a large macronucleus and one or more small micronuclei. The macronucleus controls the normal metabolism of the cell. The macronucleus disintegrates and the micronucleus undergoes meiosis. Two ciliates then exchange a haploid micronucleus.The micronuclei give rise to a new macronucleus containing certain housekeeping genes.

- *Paramecium* is by no means the only ciliate, merely one of the most common ones students will encounter during a laboratory session. Other ciliates include:
- *Blepharisma*, shown with other ciliates in Figure 13, is a ciloiate very similar to, but slower than, *Paramecium*.

- *Stentor,* a ciliate that resembles a giant blue vase with stripes.
- *Vorticella,* a stalked ciliate bearing a ring of cilia at its "mouth".

**Phylum Pyrrophyta**

The phylum Pyrrophyta contains about 1,000 species of dinoflagellates. Members of this group have cell walls and store excess sugar as starch. These organisms are surrounded by protective cellulose plates. Some dinoflagellates also are "armored", having numerous plates that cover the cell. Ornamentation on these plates can be quite beautiful.

Most dinoflagellates have two flagella; one lies in a longitudinal groove and acts as a rudder, the other is located within a transverse groove and its beating causes the cell to spin as it moves forward.

Most dinoflagellates are autotropic, having chlorophyll *a*, chlorophyll *c* in their chloroplasts, as well as a unique pigment peridinin, and some carotenoid pigments. Not all dinoflagellates are authotrophs, some are heterotrophic. Dinoflagellates can be extremely numerous, with concentrations being measured up to 30,000 individuals per cubic millimeter. Dinoflagellates are therefore an important source of food in certain ecosystems.

Certain dinoflagellates live symbiotically inside corals, and are known as zooxanthellae. The coral animal provides a sheltered space, while the dinoflagellate provides food and oxygen to its host. Zoxanthellae are the small golden brown "dots" in the coral animals.

Cell division in dinoflagellates differs from most protistans, with chromosomes attaching to the nuclear envelope and being pulled apart as the nuclear envelope stretches. During cell division in most other eukaryotes, the nuclear envelope dissolves during Prophase and reforms during Telophase.

Red tides are oceanic phenomena caused by population explosions of certain types of dinoflagellates that release a neurotoxin into the environment after they die. Shellfish concentrate this toxin into a high enough dose that it can kill people who have eaten the contaminated shellfish.

Fish kills have been linked to the dinoflagellate *Pfiesteria*. This organism does not release neurotoxins into the environment ala a red tide, but rather seesm to swarm onto fish. The lesions thus formed by the predation by the plethora of attacking *Pfiesteria*, result in the death of the fish. In certain areas of the U.S. east coast outbreaks of this organism (and other related forms) have resulted in mass fish kills.

The fossil record of dinoflagellates is excellent, with most palynologists accepting fossils from the Triassic as representing some stage of the dinoflagellate life history. The oldest fossil that might be a dinoflagellate cyst is *Arpylorus antiquus*, from the Silurian-aged rocks. A group of microfossils that may in part be dinoflagellate cysts are the hystrichospherids, some of which date from the precambrian. Acritarchs, an abundant group of precambrian and Paleozoic microfossils, may also in part be dinoflagellates or might also represent some other group of algae.

## PHYLUM APICOMPLEXA

This group consists of parasitic organisms united by their possession of a unique apical complex of microtubules. Many of the organisms now placed in this group were classified in the old Phylum Sporozoa. As a group, they have complex life cycles with diverse forms at different stages.

Members of this group cause malaria and toxoplasmosis. The life history of each organism has it infecting a different host for part of its growth. Toxoplasmosis is transmitted from cats to humans, with between 7 and 72% of the population infected, depending on the geographic area.

Malaria is a disease that effects an estimated 300 million people woreldwide. Therer are several organisms that cause malaria. most of which are spread by mosquitoes, transfusions, and shared hypodermic needles. Control of mosquito populations has led to declines in malaria in many areas. Infected individuals can be treated with a variety of medicines. However, some of the organisms that cause malaria heve developed immunity to some of the more commonly employed medicines.

*Plasmodium vivax*, the cause of one type of malaria is the most widespread human parasite. If a person is bitten by a female *Anopheles* mosquito, the parasite eventually invades the person's red blood cells. Chills and fever appear when red blood cells burst and release toxin into the person's blood.

**Phylum Sarcodina: Amoebae**

The amoeboids are in the phylum Sarcodina, which includes approximately 40,000 species. They engulf their prey with pseudopods, cytoplasmic extensions formed as cytoplasm streams in one direction. Traditional;ly this group has included the amoebas, foraminifera, and radiolaria; some of which have been removed to other groups due to recent studies.

Many amoeboids have shells, as do the foraminifera and radiolaria. *Amoeba proteus*, is a commonly studied member. When amoeboids feed, they phagocytize their food; the pseudopods surround and engulf a prey item. Digestion then occurs within a food vacuole. Freshwater amoeboids, including *Amoeba proteus*, have contractile vacuoles used to eliminate excess water.

*Entamoeba hystolitica* is an intestinal parasite in humans that causes amoebic dysentery (also known as Montezuma's Revenge or the Aztec Two-step). It is present in the water supply of many communities in Mexico (and other countries), and unless specifically filtered, toxins from this amoeba will cause a disease that can ruin a vacation. Over time, your body will acclimate to the toxins, but since many of us only are exposed for short times, our bodies will not be able to cope. Drinking filtered water should prevent contacting this illness.

*Amoeba* moves by extensions of their cytoplasm known as pseudopodia. Pseudopodia are used by many cells, and are not fixed structures like flagella but rather are associated with actin near the moving edge of the cytoplasm.

*Foraminifera* (forams) are protists that live in the oceans and secrete a shell (also known as a test) composed of silica or calcium carbonate. The cytoplasm of formals extends out from under the shell. Thus, the fossil record of forams is quite good. Oxygen isotope data from forams has been used to calculate ocean temperature fluctuations over the past 100,000 years.

## Algae

Algae are a polyphyletic group (therefore lacking any formal taxonomic validity, but still a useful term) that includes several smaller monophytletic groups. The fossil record of algae dates to the precambrian time (possible algae have been recovered from the Bitter Springs Formation rocks dated to between 1.2 and 1.4 billion years old), with undeniable algae appearing during the Paleozoic Era, by about 500 million years ago.

Most algae use photosynthesis at least part of the time. Algae are subdivided by their type of wall, photosynthetic pigments, and method of food storage. Photosynthetic pigments and storage of sugars are quite diverse within the algae. Algae are major components of the phytoplankton, an important source of oxygen and the base of many food webs in the oceans and freshwater. Body styles range from single-celled to colonial (possibly simple multicellular).

## Kingdom Stramenopila

This proposed kingdom includes the diatoms, golden algae, brown algae, and water molds. All members of this kingdom have numerous hair-like projections from their flagellae. The monophyletic nature of this group has been established by molecular systematic methods. When they are photosynthetic, chlorophyll *c* is the main accessory pigment. This kingdom includes diatoms, giant kelps, and mildews, making it a very diverse group both in terms of lifestyle as well as the size iof organisms.

## Phylum Chrysophyta

This group of freshwater, marine, and terrestrial algae includes the golden algae. Although most members of this group are autotrophs, the vast majority of them can become heterotrophs when light levels are low. Food is stored as oils, and photosynthetic pigments include chlorophyll *a* and *c* and yellow carotenoid pigments.

This phylum includes several distinct groups, some of which may be removed to other phyla in the future, such as the silicoflagellates and yellow-green algae.

## Phylum Bacillarophyta: Diatoms Live in Glass Houses

Some classifications include this phylum in the chrysophytes. Diatoms are the most numerous unicellular algae in the oceans. They are extremely numerous and an important source of food and $O_2$ for heterotrophs in aquatic systems. Examples of the various types of diatoms are shown in Figure 20. Diatoms have a cell wall comnprised of two halves technically referred to as valves. These valves are mostly made of silica ($SiO_2$). The diatom cell wall is perforated by numerous small openings. When diatoms reproduce asexually, each received one old valve. The new valve fits inside the old one; therefore, the new diatom is smaller than the original one. Once the shells reach a certain size the diatom reproduces sexually and restores its size, allowing the asexual reproduction cycle to begin anew.

Diatoms secrete a silicon dioxide shell (called a frustule) that forms the fossil deposits known as diatomaceous earth, which is used in filters and as abrasives in polishing compounds. Diatoms divide into two groups,the pennaleans with bilateral symmetry and elongated shape, and another, the centraleans, with radial symmetry and a rotund shape. Certain diatoms also are important indicators of water quality, while others are useful fossils for age-dating Quaternary deposits.

## PHYLUM PHAEOPHYTA: THE BROWN ALGAE

The phylum Phaeophyta, commonly referred to as the brown algae, are a group that is entirely multicellular. All of its members also have the accessory pigment fucoxanthin (a brown pigment that gives the group its name) and stored sugar as the carbohydrate laminarin. The chloroplasts contain both chlorophylls *a* and *c* . Members of the group include the giant kelp that can be over 100 meters long. Brown algae are used in foods, animal feeds, and fertilizers and as a source for alginate, a chemical emulsifier added to ice cream, salad dressing, and candy. Brown algae also provide food and habitat for marine organisms, as witnessed by the great biodiversity found among the kelp "forests" off the California coast.

*Fucus* is a brown alga differentiated into a floating "blade", flotation bladder, stalk (or stipe) and basal holdfast. *Sargassum*, common in the Sargasso Sea region of the Atlantic Ocean, floats and maintains position by a flotation bladder filled with gas. *Laminaria* is a kelp found in the intertidal zone. It is unique among protists because it has tissue differentiation.

**Phylum Oomycota: The Water Molds**

The phylum Oomycota includes the water molds with about 580 species. As indicated by the name, once this group was considered to belong to the fungi. Aquatic water molds parasitize fishes, forming furry growths on their gills. Some terrestrial water molds parasitize insects and plants; water mold was responsible for Irish potato famine. The body of water molds is filamentous, although cell walls are largely composed of cellulose (fungi have chitin in their cell walls). During asexual reproduction, they produce diploid motile spores (2n zoospores; most fungi lack motile spores). Unlike fungi, the adult phase of the life cycle is diploid, producing gametes by meiosis. Eggs are produced in enlarged structures known as oogonia.

**The Irish Problem**

The Irish potato famine was a terrible disaster caused by a water mold, *Phytophthora infestans*. This scourge is an example of the impact that a disease can have on the political, economic and social structure of several countries. The potato is a crop imported from South America. The potato was planted in Ireland, and the population of Ireland exploded from 4.5 million in 1800 to about 8 million in 1845. Most of the Irish were dependent on the potato for their food for ten months of the year. The late blight of potato thus had a very serious consequence to the Irish: famine and starvation. Between 1845 and 1860 over one million Irish died as a result of the famine brought about by the blight. During the same timespan, another 1.5 million emigrated, mostly to the east coast of the United States. Among immigrants during this time were ancestors of Presidents Kennedy and Reagan, among many others.

**Kingdom Rhodophyta, the Red Algae**

The red algae are placed in their own kingdom, the Rhodophyta, consisting of about 4,000 species. They are chiefly marine, multicellular organisms that are, as a rule, smaller and more delicate that the brown algae. Some are filamentous, but most are branched, having a feathery, flat, or ribbonlike appearance. Sexual reproduction involves oogamy, although the sperm are not flagellated. The food reserve is floridean starch, a polysaccharide that resembles glycogen.

Red algae have large amounts of the red pigment phycoerythrin, and range from unicellular to multicellular in their body plans (sometimes attaining greater than one meter in length). Red algae are thought to have originated by symbiosis of cyanobacteria (which also have phycoerythrin).

Some red algae, the coralline algae, are important contributors to tropical reefs. Mucilaginous material in cell walls is source of agar used to make drug capsules, dental impressions, and cosmetics. Agar is also a major microbiological media, and when purified, is a gel for electrophoresis. Agar is also used in food preparation to keep baked goods from drying and to set jellies, and desserts. Carrageenan is an additive to puddings and ice creams; dried sheets of red algae are used in some Japanese dishes.

**Chlorophyta, the "Green Algae"**

The green algae is not a real taxonomic group: it is a paraphyletic group in need to separation. There seem to be two main lineages within the traditional green algae, and these may turn out to make good monophyletic groups in future systematic revisions of the green algae. Some of the traditional green algae should remain in the Chlorophyta, while others that are allied with plants should be removed to the Plant Kingdom. Pending such a revision, present the green algae as if they were in fact monophyletic, but with full realization they are not. Confused? Green algae have cellulose cell walls, both chlorophylls *a* and *b*, and store excess sugar as starch. Some mebers of this group have been considered the undoubted ancestors of plants. Not all members of this group are allied to the plants, however. Body types in the green algae include unicellular to colonial as well as simple multicelluar. We will examine several of these representative groups.

*Chlamydomonas,* and similar cells appear to be a starting point within this group. Autotrophic, unicellular forms with a single, cup-shaped chloroplast and two apically inserted flagella, these small cells also possess a contractile vacuole and pyrenoid. Excess sugars are stored as starch surrounding the pyrenoid.

*Chlamydomonas* reproduces sexually when growth conditions are unfavorable, a common process employed by many protists to withstand or outlast a deteriorating environment. Gametes from two different mating types (since this organism is typically isogamous we cannot use the terms male and female) come into contact and join to form a diploid zygote. A heavy wall forms around the zygote, in effect turning the diploid zygote into a resistant zygospore that can survive until conditions become favorable once again.

Multicellular green algae have some division of labor, producing various reproductive cells and structures. The common sea lettuce is usually haploid (the gametophyte) and reproduces asexually. Gametes are produced by mitosis, fuse, and produce a diploid zygote. The 2n zygote germinates and grows to become the sporophyte. Meiosis occurs in certain of the cells in the sporophyte, producing haploid swimming spores that will settle to the ocean floor and produce the next generation haploid gametophyte stage.

Filametous algae produce gametes by mitosis within one cell of the filament. These gametes are released, fuse to form a diploid zygote that soon undergoes meiosis to produce hapoid zoospores that swim, rest on the sea floor and develop into the next generation gametophyte phase.

*Lvox* cells resemble a *Chlamydomonas* cell. A new colony arises as if daughter cells fail to separate.

## SLIME MOLDS: MYXOMYCOTA

Slime molds are often classified as fungi, although now most specialists consider them a group of protistans. In y related to other groups of plants or animals. Slime molds, which spend part of their life as single-celled forms, can aggregate to form multicellular forms. They thus may represent a transition between unicellular and multicelluar forms, the second major advancement after the evolution of eukaryotic cells.

### The Fossil Record

The first protist fossils occur in rocks approximatly 1.2-1.4 billion years old from the Bitter Springs Formation in Australia. However, some paleobiologists doubt that these small (a mere 5 micrometers in diameter) cells are actually eukaryotic. An older group of eukaryotic microfossils (perhaps dating back as far as 1.8 billion years ago) are the acritarchs. Many "algae" produce resting cysts that resemble acritarchs. Multicellular protists appeared in the fossil record more than 600 million years ago. Some problemmatic fossils, thought by some paleobotanists to be algae, have been found in rocks approximately one billion years old.

# Chapter–4

# Heterotrophic Protists

## INTRODUCTION

It has been recognised for many years that variation in the rate at which primary production is converted to zooplankton biomass is quite large. Some aquatic food webs, such as found in many hypereutrophic lakes, have very high biomass of primary producers, but relatively low zooplankton and fish biomasses, as demonstrated by the Eltonian biomass pyramids. Other systems, such as marine upwelling zones, are low in phytoplankton biomass, but have very high zooplankton and fish biomasses This variation in carbon transfer efficiency can be attributed to variation in food quality.

The food quality of a planktonic prey organism is given by a combination of factors including morphological, physiological, behavioural, chemical, and biochemical features. Additionally, particular requirements of the consumer together with its ability to ingest and digest the prey organism contribute to the determination of the ultimate quality of a planktonic prey. The nutritional value of prey organisms is more specifically determined by the prey mineral and biochemical composition as well as by the efficiency of a consumer in assimilating prey minerals and essential biochemical compounds. It is well known, that some cyanobacteria species (blue-green algae), despite their reported edibility for zooplankton in many cases, are a poor food, primarily attributed to phosphorus limitation. On the other hand, phytoplankton species may be neither phosphorus nor nitrogen limited, but lack biochemical compounds, which are essential for herbivorous predators. Most of the biochemical compounds, which have been considered in studies of nutritional quality in aquatic food webs, are lipids (fatty acids and sterols) or proteins (especially essential amino acids).

The high-energy content of lipids relative to proteins or carbohydrates coupled with the small body size of most planktonic invertebrates makes lipids the energy storage biomolecules of choice for zooplankton. Zooplankton lipids often comprise 60–65% of their dry weight, and their cellular function depends on the molecular structure (Fig. 4.1). Triacylglycerols and phospholipids are biochemically related, as they have a glycerol backbone to which two or three fatty acids are esterified . Triacylglycerols are very important energy storage molecules, whereas phospholipids are essential components of membranes. Sterols share with phospholipids a structural function in membranes, but in terms of polarity they are grouped with triacylglycerols in the neutral lipids. Phospholipids are grouped with polar lipids, including glycolipids. Glycolipids contain one or more molecules of a sugar and are found in bacteria, plants, and animals.

Among lipid molecules, fatty acids have received considerable attention, because they are usually present in low amounts but serve very important physical and metabolic functions ]in the cell. Especially highly unsaturated fatty acids (HUFA) of the ?3 and ?6 families, like eicosapentaenoic acid ) and docosahexaenoic acid as well as some polyunsaturated fatty acids (PUFA), like arachidonic acid (20:4?6) and linoleic acid (18:2?6) are considered essential for many zooplanktonic consumers, which are not able to synthesize fatty acids. Enhanced growth and reproduction of cladocerans, especially Daphnia, have been associated with higher contents of HUFA and PUFA in cultured prey organisms.

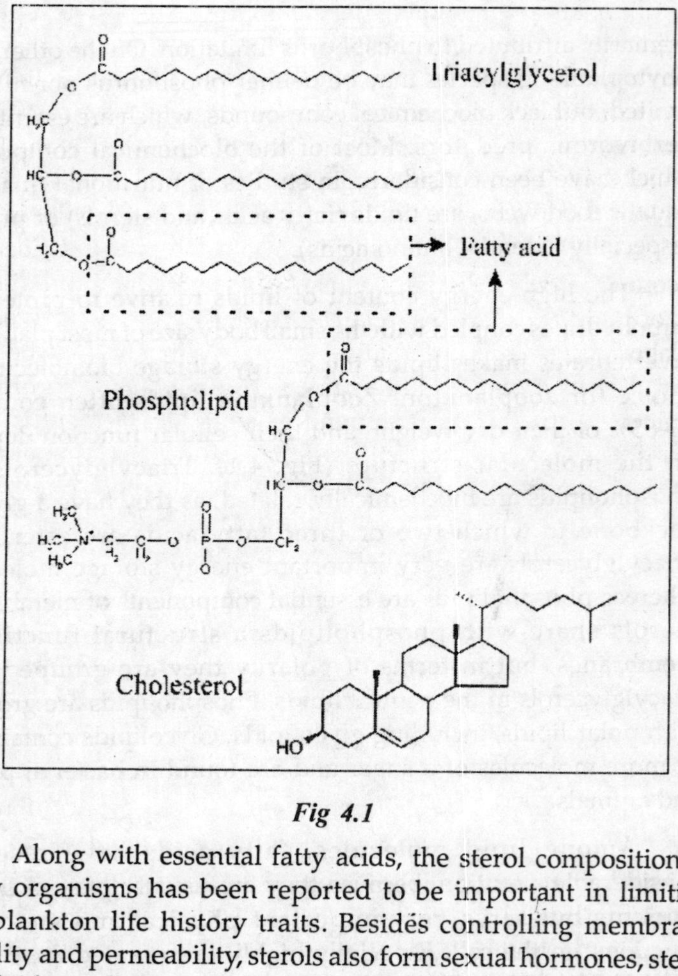

Triacylglycerol

Fatty acid

Phospholipid

Cholesterol

*Fig 4.1*

Along with essential fatty acids, the sterol composition of prey organisms has been reported to be important in limiting zooplankton life history traits. Besidés controlling membrane fluidity and permeability, sterols also form sexual hormones, sterol alkaloids, and act as vitamins. Sterol limitation for growth and reproduction of zooplankton predators has been found to be mainly caused by dietary cholesterol shortage, which has been associated with decreased growth of copepods and cladocerans, and retarded larval development of crustaceans .

Amino acids are the basic structural unit of protein molecules. Some amino acids cannot be synthesized by animal cells at all or only at low rates. These amino acids are considered essential and must therefore be supplied in the diet.

There is an ongoing debate on the factors, which primarily determine the nutritional quality of a planktonic prey for its consumer – the mineral or the biochemical composition. Some authors have advocated the relevance of prey mineral composition and elemental stoichiometry, especially the P:C and N:C ratios, in determining prey nutritional quality, because mineral nutrients usually limit production and growth in nature. Others have emphasized the importance of essential biochemical compounds in promoting enhanced growth and reproduction of zooplankton, based on correlative evidences derived from laboratory and in situ studies. Actually, elements may be present in a wide range of biochemical compounds. Therefore, the biochemistry of the compound in which an element is present dictates how that element is processed by a consumer. Hence, the concept of elemental stoichiometry, although powerful and useful, may not be sufficient to the full understanding of the food-related limitation of zooplankton production.

Further, there is a controversy on the question, which biochemical compound is most important in limiting zooplankton life-history traits. Some authors showed evidence for the essentiality of the polyunsaturated fatty acid EPA for Daphnia, while others did not find any limitation by EPA on daphniids and suggested that sterols may be more important lipids limiting Daphnia growth. Moreover, DHA and linoloenic acid have been reported to limit growth and reproduction of zooplankton. It must be kept in mind that nutritional quality is not only a matter of prey composition, but also of predator requirements. The fact that EPA was found to limit Daphnia growth under a set of conditions does not necessarily imply limitation under different conditions. This does not mean that EPA is not limiting at all, but that its limitation may be modulated by other factors, which were not quantified. Living organisms are actually a complex "package" of nutrients interacting on molecular, biochemical, and physiological levels. Thus, prey organisms should be viewed as a dynamic pool of nutrients rather than as a static source of unaltered composition waiting to be eaten.

## THE SIGNIFICANCE OF HETEROTROPHIC PROTISTS IN AQUATIC FOOD WEBS

It is known that a large fraction of the primary production may not be consumed directly by herbivorous consumers but is channelled through detrital organic matter via bacterial production to phagotrophic microrganisms. This led to the concept of the "microbial loop" and to the discovery that planktonic food chains include a higher number of trophic levels than hitherto believed.

However, recent works have shown that the early view of the microbial loop was somehow too simplistic. Today we know that: heterotrophic bacteria do not only rely on dissolved organic matter (DOM) released by autotrophs as a substrate, but also on DOM released by heterotrophs (Jumars et al., 1989); heterotrophic protists comprise more than one trophic level, as predation of ciliates on flagellates is also known; grazing by protists may not simply affect bacterial numbers but also have an impact on the morphological structure and productivity of bacterial communities; there are immense species-specific differences concerning the trophic roles of protists in a food web; some flagellates, for instance, show autotrophic, mixotrophic and heterotrophic growth under natural conditions ; the production of low trophic levels is not only channelled to higher trophic levels through consumption of bacterial biomass by ciliates and flagellates; but that herbivory by heterotrophic protists also contributes significantly to the matter transfer to higher trophic levels. Therefore interactions of heterotrophic protists in planktonic food webs are more various and complex than traditionally believed. The use of simplified "chains" or "loops" does not capture the complexity of microbial food webs.

Several laboratorial studies with cultured protists have shown that mesozooplankton predators are able to efficiently grow and reproduce on a diet consisting of heterotrophic protists. Moreover, heterotrophic protists are likely to be an important alternative food resource for zooplankton when phytoplankton abundances are low or when phytoplankton quality is reduced (e.g. during periods of nutrient limitation). High predation pressure by copepods and cladocerans has been observed as a mechanism regulating protist community structure and densities in situ. However, evidence for high predation rates by mesozooplankton on heterotrophic protists does not attribute them high nutritional quality. Unfortunately, little attention has been paid to the biochemical features of heterotrophic protists, which do confer their nutritional value as prey in aquatic food webs.

## THE NUTRITIONAL COMPOSITION OF HETEROTROPHIC PROTISTS

Most of the information on the nutritional composition of heterotrophic protists dates back to the 60s and 70s, mostly related to studies of the ciliate Tetrahymena. It is well known that heterotrophic protists often have lower C:N ratios than algae and mixotrophic protists. The lower C:N ratios suggest that heterotrophic protists may be a source of nitrogen-rich compounds such as amino acids and proteins. Nevertheless, the amino acid composition of free-living heterotrophic protists is virtually unknown, except for studies on Tetrahymena.

It is has been observed that the fatty acid composition of heterotrophic protists is strongly influenced by the food resources. However, there are too few studies on the fatty acid composition of heterotrophic protists to permit such a generalization. Indeed, synthesis of long-chain polyunsaturated fatty acids has been reported for marine flagellates, suggesting that this metabolic ability should not be excluded for other species.

Despite studies on marine species, the sterol composition of freshwater heterotrophic protists is still a 'black box'. The only exceptions are studies on freshwater flagellates of the genus Chilomonas, for which 24α-ethylcholesta-5,22(E)-dien-3ß-ol (stigmasterol) was described as the predominant sterol, and the bacterivorous ciliate Tetrahymena pyiriformis, for which a triterpenoid alcohol – tetrahymanol (gammaceran-3ß-ol) – was first isolated and described as its major neutral lipid.

It has been observed that the biochemical composition of heterotrophic protists resembles dietary composition. For bacterivorous ciliates a fatty acid profile typical for bacteria has been reported, with high concentrations of odd chain-length and branched fatty acids. Algivorous protists, in turn, have been reported to show a broader spectrum of polyunsaturated fatty acids, which are not typically found in bacteria. However, some authors reported the presence of compounds in heterotrophic species, which were not identified in their diet. The question remains, whether or not heterotrophic protists "are really what they eat", or if they are able to metabolize some compounds obtained from the diet, thus modifying their biochemical composition (heterotrophic protists "are not what they eat").

Some protist species have a fascinatingly complex nutritional ecology. Some flagellated species are able to adapt to a broad range of external conditions, because they exhibit a wide range of trophic modes, such as autotrophy, heterotrophy, and mixotrophy. Assuming that the trophic mode will ultimately determine the nutritional composition of such species, a large variability in the biochemical composition is expected to be found in these protists. As autotrophs, they are able to synthesize a broad palette of compounds, which are necessary for growth and maintenance. As heterotrophs, they ingest particulate material (phagotrophy) or absorb (osmotrophy) a wide diversity of molecules from their environment, thus extracting organic and inorganic building blocks for their own biosynthesis reactions as well as energy for growth and maintenance. As mixotrophs, phagotrophy or osmotrophy supplements photosynthesis to generate energy and provide carbohydrate building blocks.

The nutritional complexity of protists raises interesting questions about the nature of the mechanisms, which influence their biochemical composition, and subsequent nutritional quality as prey. Does the biochemical composition of protists depend only on their trophic mode? And within the same trophic mode, e.g. heterotroph/phagotroph, are there differences between algivores and bacterivores, i.e. does the dietary composition determine protist biochemical composition? Between two algivores fed the same algae, are there species-specific differences in the biochemical composition? Those questions should be answered before one decides to evaluate the nutritional quality of protists for zooplankton predators. Only by knowing the biochemical composition of protists and to which extent it can be dictated by dietary composition or by the trophic mode, it is possible to evaluate what really determines the nutritional quality of protists as prey for planktonic predators.

## OUTLINE OF THE THESIS AND HYPOTHESES

To evaluate the influence of the biochemical composition of heterotrphic protists on their nutritional quality as prey I performed population gro he nutritional value of heterotrophic protists for rotifers. The rotifer was offered the four protist species and the biochemical composition of the protists was correlated to population growth rates and to the cumulative number of eggs produced by *K. quadrata* during the experiments.

The last question was formulated found evidence for the potential of some biochemicals of the protists to limit egg production of the rotifers. To test the effect of single biochemical compounds directly I artificially supplementated one protist species – *Chilomonas paramecium* – with two selected polyunsaturated fatty acids (EPA and DHA) and evaluated the effect of supplemented versus non-supplemented flagellates on population growth and egg production of *K. quadrata*.

To address this hypothesis, selected four species, which were fed different diets: the algivorous ciliates Balanion planctonicum and Urotricha farcta were fed the cryptomonad Cryptomonas phasmecium were fed bacteria grown on rice corns. The fatty acid and amino acid composition as well as the sterol compositio were analysed in both the protists and their diet. Discrepancies between protist and dietary biochemical composition are discussed in light of metabolic features of the protists. Differences between two species fed the same diet are discussed in terms of species-specific metabolic features of the protists.

The trophic mode determines the biochemical composition of the flagellate *Ochromonas* sp.

To test this hypothesis, the fatty acid and sterol composition of the flagellate Ochromonas sp. grown as autotroph, mixotroph, and heterotroph was analysed. The role of photosynthesis and phagotrophy in determining metabolic patterns of fatty acid and sterol synthesis and accumulation are discussed.

Heterotrophic protists fed different diets have different nutritional quality for a rotifer predator due to differences in their biochemical compounds.

To test this hypothesis, the rotifer *K. quadrata* was separately offered two algivorous and two bacterivorous protists as prey . The cryptomonad *C. phaseolus* was used as a good quality control food. The biochemical composition of the protists, which was analysed in the previous chapters, was correlated with population growth rates and the egg numbers of the rotifer.

Chilomonas paramecium can be sucesssfully supplemented with essential fatty acids (EPA and DHA), in order to test the influence of these biochemicals on rotifers' life-history traits.

Correlation analyses between prey biochemical composition and the cumulative number of eggs produced by the rotifer *K. quadrata,* provided evidence for limiting effects of EPA and DHA, among other compounds. I tested a new supplementation technique for supplementing the heterotrophic flagellate *Chilomonas paramecium* with EPA and DHA. Up to now, this supplementation technique has been only used for supplementing algal cells. The efficiency of the method was tested by supplementing *C. paramecium* with different EPA and DHA incubation concentrations. To test whether the nutritional quality of *C. paramecium* was enhanced through EPA and DHA supplementation, the effects of supplemented versus non-supplemented *Chilomonas* on population growth rates and egg numbers of the rotifer *K. quadrata* were evaluated.

Aquatic food webs rely on autotrophs as these are the most important resource of essential chemical components for the mesozooplankton. Heterotrophic protists on the other hand are an important trophic link in aquatic food webs, as they prey on primary producers and bacteria, and are themselves preyed upon by the mesozooplankton. Depending on their ability to assimilate and incorporate chemical compounds obtained from their diet, heterotrophic protists have the potential to modify the chemical composition of organic matter at an early stage in the food chain.

In zooplankton species, the fatty acid composition of a predator usually resembles that of its prey. Daphnia galeata exhibited higher concentrations of the polyunsaturated fatty acids EPA (eicosapenenoic acid) and DHA (docosahexaenoic acid) when fed a cryptomonad than *D. galeata* fed green algae. Similarly, *Acartia tonsa* exhibited higher concentrations of saturated and monounsaturated fatty acids when fed a bacterivorous ciliate and higher concentrations of polyunsaturated fatty acids when fed diatoms. A study involving two marine ciliates showed that the lipid composition (fatty acids, neutral lipids, and sterols) of the ciliates resembled that of their prey (either bacteria or algae). Assuming that these findings are also valid for freshwater heterotrophic protists, one would expect differences in the chemical make-up of heterotrophic protists fed different diets. Indeed, bacterivorous protists contained large amounts of saturated (SAFA) and monounsaturated (MUFA) fatty acids (together comprising more than 85% of the total fatty acids), and very low quantities of polyunsaturated fatty acids (PUFA), and highly unsaturated fatty acids (HUFA). In contrast, algivorous ciliates are expected to contain high quantities of PUFA, HUFA, and some essential amino acids. In algivorous marine ciliates, SAFA and PUFA comprised 32% and 57% of the total fatty acids. The amino acid composition of mesozooplankton predators seems to be rather constant, and more or less independent of the amino acid composition of their diet. Except for studies on Tetrahymena, the amino acid composition of freshwater heterotrophic protists is virtually unknown.

Different protist species may show different metabolic features. To date little is known about species-specific differences in fatty acid and amino acid metabolism of freshwater heterotrophic protist species. Such differences are expected to occur and may contribute to the transfer of essential compounds between primary producers and higher level consumers in aquatic food webs. In addition to the assimilation and incorporation of dietary compounds, de novo synthesis of some essential compounds has been observed in ciliates and flagellates. The bacterivorous ciliate Pleuronema sp. was found to contain high concentrations of a triterpenoid alcohol (tetrahymanol), as a major neutral lipid, which was not observed in its bacterial prey. Also the ability of the heterotrophic dinoflagellate Oxyrrhis marina to synthesize EPA, DHA, and some sterols has already been described.

We now address the question of how the biochemical profile (fatty acids and essential amino acids) of freshwater heterotrophic protists reflects that of their diet. Furthermore, we looked for differences in the biochemical composition between protist species fed the same diet. To elucidate the relationship between the biochemical composition of heterotrophic protists and their diet, we compare the fatty acid and essential amino acid composition of four protist species with the fatty acid and essential amino acid composition of their diet. The ciliates Balanion planctonicum and *Urotricha farcta* were cultured on the cryptomonad *Cryptomonas phaseolus* and the ciliate *Cyclidium* sp. and the flagellate *Chilomonas paramecium* were cultured on a mixed diet consisting of bacteria and small rice particles. Our study examines the fate of the biochemical compounds, which confer food quality to heterotrophic protists and emphasizes species-specific differences in protist ability to transform energy and organic matter at an early stage in the aquatic food web, when the disparity in the biochemical composition may be large.

# Chapter–5

# Plankton Samples and Radiolarian Study

## INTRODUCTION

Plankton samples for radiolarian studies are usually collected with nets. However, this group, as well as a few other microzooplanktonic taxa, pose serious methodological difficulties. Indeed, they are too small (around 20-30 to 300 µm) to collect effectively with standard zooplanktonic nets (100 to 300 µm in pore size), yet too scarce in most areas to yield adequate catches with water-bottles or low-powered pumps. Thus, fine-meshed nets have to be employed, which significantly complicates not only the concentration of the radiolarians (due to the concomitant retrieval of other organisms, some of which, like the diatoms, cannot be fractioned out later, but also because net clogging jeopardizes subsequent estimations of the volume of water filtered. In order to avoid clogging by smaller particles, thus ensuring better estimates of the volume of water filtered and larger sample-sizes, meshes ranging between 60 and up to 100 µm are traditionally used for polycystine studies in the water-column. It should be stressed, however, that both absolute quantitative estimates of radiolarian abundance, and the proportions of at least some species and developmental stages may be seriously biased in these collections reported that in sediment trap materials from the tropical Atlantic shells below 40-60 µm represent roughly 50% of the overall polycystine fauna.

Estimates of radiolarian abundances in the water-column must be performed with flow-metered nets; clogging of the meshes, in particular of those with small pores, makes assessment of the volume of water filtered based on distance towed and mouth diameter extremely unreliable. Thus, whenever unflowmetered nets are employed, opening-closing mechanism, it is strongly recommended that evaluation of radiolarian concentrations be avoided (species proportions, on the other hand, are in principle unaffected in these samples).

For assessment of the delicate colonial forms, as well as for studies of feeding, growth, metabolism, etc. of live individuals, specimens are collected by divers, or by means of very short and slow plankton tows, thus ensuring a better preservation of the protists.

Sediment trap techniques have undergone major improvements in the last years, thus constituting a very useful tool for the collection of polycystine materials. Simple sediment traps consist of a concentrating cone or funnel which tapers into a collecting jar; the array, which can have either one or several traps, is moored to the bottom or drifts with the current suspended from a buoy at the surface. Time-series models are deployed at different oceanic locations for periods up to a year or more, and are provided with a mechanism which replaces the collecting cup at predetermined intervals thus yielding a detailed record of the changes in the amount and type of flux throughout several seasons.

Sediment-trap materials have some important advantages over planktonic collections. Sample-size is usually much larger in sediment traps than in plankton nets, with fluxes as high as 200,000 shells/m$^2$/day having been recorded in the equatorial Atlantic. Seasonal plankton collections are composed of a sequence of snapshots which represent but an insignificant proportion of the total time elapsed between tows, and may therefore not only under- or overestimate mean protist abundances, but also yield "atypical" specific assemblages. Time-series sediment trap samples, on the other hand, integrate over preselected depth and time ranges, thus averaging the overlying plankton over restricted periods which yield adequate chronological resolution to allow pinpointing the relative importance of limited offsets of the yearly cycle. Furthermore, since seasonal variations in total mass flux are usually closely coupled with primary production in the upper mixed layer, comparison of total flux vs. radiolarian numbers and specific makeup can furnish first hand information on indicators (and paleoindicators) of the biological productivity of the associated water masses.

Sediment trap materials, however, also have some shortcomings. Because of limitations associated with the hydrodynamic properties of particle accumulation in the traps, these devices are most effective when deployed at depths in excess of 500-700 m. As a result, they integrate the flux from several biologically dissimilar layers. Furthermore, sinking skeletons intercepted at these depths may not adequately reflect their standing stocks at the surface, nor their specific composition. In the Weddell Sea, over 90% of the polycystines that inhabit the upper 400 m are destroyed (probably due to fragmentation by grazing) before reaching 400-900 m of depth.

Subsurface advection of shells produced at higher latitudes and integration of low protist abundances over large depth intervals may be responsible for the fact that, in the eastern equatorial Atlantic, polycystine assemblage compositions recorded in plankton samples at 0-300 m are totally different from those recovered in traps at 800-2000 m.

It should be borne in mind that the yields of sediment trap samples are not amenable to direct comparisons with those of plankton samples: while the former are an expression of the downward flux, which in turn is associated with productivity and preservation, quantitative plankton samples give information on standing stock only. Hence, compositional differences may not only reflect advection, destruction by grazing, etc., but also biological traits of the species considered. Thus, a scarce species with high reproduction, mortality and output rates may be rare in the plankton but abundant in the underlying sediment trap.

As with other zooplanktonic groups, analyses of radiolarian vertical distribution patterns are usually performed with the aid of vertically stratified plankton tows. However, because their identification is based on the siliceous skeleton which preserves after the death of the cell, in order to discriminate live vs. dead protists in the subsurface layers the cytoplasm is often stained with Rose Bengal, Sudan black B, or eosin. Although this technique can furnish some clues on the living depth ranges of the species, it does not provide unequivocal information because of uncertainties associated with the speed of decomposition of the protists' cytoplasm. Specimens of several planktonic foraminifera still contained protoplasm in their shell 98 days after death. The proportions of presumably live benthic Foraminifera as indicated by Rose Bengal and Sudan black B staining and by ATP assay, concluding that stained protoplasm was present in individuals up to four weeks after actual death of the cell. These lapses are significantly longer than the time it takes a radiolarian shell to reach the sea-floor.

Unless special cytological studies are required, plankton and sediment trap samples can be preserved in 4-5% formaldehyde; the addition of picric acid to the solution enhances the preservation of the colonies, yet acidification should be avoided if the calcareous plankton is to be saved from dissolution.

## SAMPLE PREPARATION AND ANALYSIS

The following section offers some general comments on the preparation of whole samples for routine counting and identification procedures. It does not review the methods involved in special cytological and ultrastructural studies (see Anderson 1983a, for a review of these topics), as well as those used for detailed taxonomic work, which can involve thin-sectioning, etching and polishing, etc.

Pelagic surface sediments are usually clean enough as to require little treatment before preparation of the slides. Elimination of the organic matter and disaggregation of the materials is achieved by boiling the sample (5-10 g) for a few minutes in a beaker with water to which hydrogen peroxyde (10%,

300 ml per litre) and tetrasodium pyrophosphate (10 g per litre) have been added. Disaggregation, cleaning and removal of clay coatings and infilling particles can be aided by treating the sample in a gentle ultrasonic bath. For further disaggregation of heavily indurated sediments various products, such as kerosene, paint thinner, or ammonia can be helpful (the sediment is dried, soaked in the solvent, and then immersed in water, upon which disaggregation usually occurs rapidly). If calcareous material is abundant it can be removed with a few drops of hydrochloric acid (after eliminating the hydrogen peroxyde by wet-sieving). The resulting clean material is then sieved with abundant water in order to eliminate the reagents and smaller particles. The mesh size used depends on the aims of the study; most surveys routinely employ 40-60 μm-meshes, yet these, as described above, miss many of the smaller species, as well as most developing forms. If precise abundance estimates are sought, mesh openings around 15 to 20 μm should be employed, although these will retain large numbers of unidentifiable skeletal fragments, as well as non-radiolarian material (especially diatoms), which can make subsequent observation more laborious. The clean residue in the sieve is pipetted onto glass microscope slides, dried, and soaked with a few drops of xylene; before the xylene has evaporated the mounting medium is added and covered with a cover glass. Canada Balsam is most often used for these preparations, although it takes longer to harden than some other synthetic materials, commercially known as Norland, Pleurax, Hyrax or Depex.

The quantification of the number of radiolarian shells per unit weight of sediment. Before processing as described above, the sample is dried and weighed. This weighed sediment is then cleaned and sieved, and all the resulting residue is poured into a large (e.g., 5 litre) beaker full of distilled water, on the bottom of which one or two cover gasses have been positioned. The water with the sediment in the beaker is then thoroughly stirred (avoiding rotational motion, which will result in centrifugal fractionation) for achieving a random distribution of the particles, and the sediment is allowed to settle. With the aid of a siphon all but 30-50 mm of water are removed, and the remainder is evaporated with an overhead infrared lamp. When the surface of the cover glasses is dry they are removed from the beaker and mounted as described above. The slide thus prepared will contain a fraction of the radiolarian shells present in the original sample, this fraction being equivalent to the proportion that the surface of the cover glass makes of that of the surface of the bottom of the beaker.

Preparation of plankton and sediment trap samples is somewhat more laborious due to the large amounts of organic material they contain. When both absolute radiolarian concentrations and specific inventories are sought, it is recommended that counting be performed separately from the identifications. Polycystines can be counted (although not identified) in whole, unprocessed samples in counting chambers under the inverted microscope. Subsequently, either the entire sample or a subsample can be treated in order to eliminate all organic matter leaving the clean siliceous skeletons that will be mounted as described above for sedimentary materials. It should be born in mind, however, that radiolarian cells are often very difficult to recognize in preserved, unprocessed plankton samples. The siliceous skeleton, usually the most conspicuous distinguishing feature, is obscured by the cytoplasm to such an extent that radiolarians are easily confused with other planktonic protists, fecal pellets, eggs, various organic aggregates, debris, etc. Adding a few drops of hydrogen peroxide and/or hydrochloric acid, which slowly digest the organic matter, and comparing the dubious particles before and after treatment can greatly help to pinpoint radiolarian cells.

Several different methods have been used for eliminating organic material from water-column samples, including high- and low-temperature ashing, oxidizing with hydrogen peroxide and/or ultraviolet light, etc. for cleaning diatom frustules. The plankton sample is rinsed with abundant fresh water (wet-sieving), and placed in a beaker to which an equal volume of saturated $KMnO_4$ is added; it is then left for 24 hs. A volume of concentrated HCl equivalent to that already contained in the beaker is subsequently added to the sample; the dark brown liquid is gently heated until it becomes transparent or light yellow. Once the sample has cooled, it is sieved again thoroughly with fresh water and rinsed with distilled water. The residue is pipetted onto microscope glass slides as described above.

## RADIOLARIAN SPECIES

Assessment of radiolarian species-specific absolute and relative abundances are based on identifications and counts. Since any given slide often contains thousands of polycystine shells, the researcher is forced to decide how many specimens should be identified and counted in order to achieve an adequate estimate of overall numbers and species proportions. Several methods have been proposed for the assessment of bias in sample-based particle counts and in the appraisal of species proportions the species representing >50% of the overall taxocoenosis at least 50 specimens should be counted in order to achieve reliable percentage data, 300 counts for species which comprise approximately 10% of a sample, 500-1000 counts for species that make up 5%, and counts of several thousands for those that comprise 1%. Unfortunately, in the case of the polycystines these efforts are unrealistic because in any given sample containing 100-150 species only one-three are above 10%, and 70-90 occur at levels below 1% (see "Geographic and vertical distribution"). In terms of the amount of information attained, it is more profitable to analyze more samples at a lower resolution, than to examine fewer sites at these statistically more reliable levels. Thus, in practice proportions are estimated in bulk, regardless of the individual pecies abundances, usually scanning 300-600 specimens per sample. It is common practice to identify the first 300-600 individuals on the slide, and then check the rest of the slide or slides for the given sample in order to account for the rarer taxa. The relative abundances of the latter are estimated approximately, and they are usually excluded from subsequent general numerical analyses (e.g., multivariate techniques, such as cluster and factor analysis) because of the uncertainties associated with their assumed absences. It should be stressed, however, that the counting effort necessary for reliable estimates of the fractional abundance of the rare species is inversely proportional to the equitability of the assemblage. Thus, when the sample is strongly dominated by a single or only a few taxa, such as in polar areas, chances of recording the rare polycystines in random sequential counts are low because the observer repeatedly hits the dominant species. On the contrary, as equitability increases so does the probability of logging a so far unrecorded species with every new specimen scanned.

# Chapter–6

# Animal and Plant like Protists

## AMOEBOID

Amoeboids are unicellular lifeforms that mainly consist of contractile vacuoles, a nucleus, and cytoplasm as their basic structure. They move and feed by means of temporary cytoplasmic projections, called pseudopods (false feet). They have appeared in a number of different groups. Some cells in multicellular animals may be amoeboid, for instance human white blood cells, which consume pathogens. Many protists also exist as individual amoeboid cells, or take such a form at some point in their life-cycle. The most famous such organism is *Amoeba proteus*; the name amoeba is variously used to describe its close relatives, other organisms similar to it, or the amoeboids in general.

### Scientific Classification

***Classes and Sub-classes***

Class Lobose pseudopods

- Amoebozoa
- Percolozoa

Class Filose pseudopods

- Cercozoa

Vampyrellids

Nucleariids

Class Reticulose pseudopods

Foraminifera

Gymnophryids

Class Actinopods

Radiolaria

Heliozoa

Foraminiferan (*Ammonia tepida*)

Heliozoan (*Actinophrys sol*)

## MORPHOLOGICAL CATEGORIES

Amoeboids may be divided into several morphological categories based on the form and structure of the pseudopods. Those where the pseudopods are supported by regular arrays of microtubules are called actinopods, and forms where they are not are called rhizopods, further divided into lobose, filose, and reticulose amoebae. There is also a strange group of giant marine amoeboids, the xenophyophores, that do not fall into any of these categories.

- **Lobose Pseudopods**

Lobose pseudopods are blunt, and there may be one or several on a cell, which is usually divided into a layer of clear ectoplasm surrounding more granular endoplasm. Most, including *Amoeba* itself, move by the body mass flowing into an anterior pseudopod. The vast majority form a monophyletic group called the Amoebozoa, which also includes most slime molds. A second group, the Percolozoa, includes protists that can transform between amoeboid and flagellate forms.

- **Filose Pseudopods**

Filose pseudopods are narrow and tapering. The vast majority of filose amoebae, including all those that produce shells, are placed within the Cercozoa together with various flagellates that tend to have amoeboid forms. The naked filose amoebae comprise two other groups, the vampyrellids and nucleariids. The latter appear to be close relatives of animals and fungi.

- **Reticulose Pseudopods**

Reticulose pseudopods are cytoplasmic strands that branch and merge to form a net. They are found most notably among the Foraminifera, a large group of marine protists that generally produce multi-chambered shells. There are only a few sorts of naked reticulose amoeboids, notably the gymnophryids, and their relationships are not certain.

- **Actinopods**

Actinopods are divided into the radiolaria and heliozoa. The radiolaria are mostly marine protists with complex internal skeletons, including central capsules that divide the cells into granular endoplasm and frothy ectoplasm that keeps them buoyant. The heliozoa include both freshwater and marine forms that use their axopods to capture small prey, and only have simple scales or spines for skeletal elements. Both groups appear to be polyphyletic.

However, amoeboids have appeared separately in many other groups, including various different lines of algae not listed above.

- **Subphylum Sarcodina**

Sarcodina is a subphylum of the phylum Sarcomastigophora, of unicellular life forms that move by cytoplasmic flow. Some species use cytoplasmic extensions called pseudopodia for locomotion or feeding. The subphylum includes such protozoa as the common amoeba and the Foraminifera and Radiolaria. Most members of the subphylum reproduce asexually through fission, although some reproduce sexually. Sarcodina is sometimes subdivided into two classes - Rhizopoda and Actinopoda.

The ciliates are one of the most important groups of protists, common almost everywhere there is water — lakes, ponds, oceans, rivers, and soils, with many ectosymbiotic and endosymbiotic members, as well as some obligate and opportunistic parasites included. Ciliates tend to be large protozoa, a few reaching 2 mm in length, and are some of the most complex in structure. The name *ciliate* comes from the presence of hair-like organelles called cilia, which are identical in structure to flagella but typically shorter and present in much larger numbers with a different undulating pattern than flagella. Cilia occur in all members of the group (although the peculiar suctoria only have them for part of the life-cycle) and are variously used in swimming, crawling, attachment, feeding, and sensation.

Unlike other eukaryotes, ciliates have two different sorts of nuclei: a small, diploid micronucleus (reproduction), and a large, polyploid macronucleus (general cell regulation). The latter is generated from the micronucleus by amplification of the genome and heavy editing. Division of the macronucleus occurs by amitosis, the segregation of the chromosomes is by a process whose mechanism is unknown. This process is by no means perfect, and after about 200 generations the cell shows signs of aging. Periodically the macronuclei must be regenerated from the micronuclei. In most, this occurs during *conjugation*. Here two cells line up, the micronuclei undergo meiosis, some of the haploid daughters are exchanged and then fuse to form new micronuclei and macronuclei.

Food vacuoles are formed through phagocytosis and typically follow a particular path through the cell as their contents are digested and broken down via lysosomes so the substances the vacuole contains are then small enough to diffuse through the membrane of the food vacuole into the cell. Anything left in the food vacuole by the time it reaches the cytoproct (anus) is discharged via exocytosis. Most ciliates also have one or more prominent contractile vacuoles, which collect water and expel it from the cell to maintain osmotic pressure, or in some function to maintain ionic balance. These often have a distinctive star-shape, with each point being a collecting tube.

## Feeding

Most ciliates feed on smaller organisms (heterotrophic), such as bacteria and algae, and detritus swept into the oral groove (mouth) by modified oral cilia. This usually includes a series of membranelles to the left of the mouth and a paroral membrane to its right, both of which arise from *polykinetids*, groups of many cilia together with associated structures. The food is moved by the cilia through the mouth pore into the gullet, which forms food vacuoles.

This varies considerably, however. Some ciliates are mouthless and feed by absorption, while others are predatory and feed on other protozoa and in particular on other ciliates. This includes the suctoria, which feed through several specialized tentacles

**Reproduction**

Ciliates can undergo both asexual and sexual reproduction. Asexual reproduction occurs by binary fission. The micronucleus undergoes by mitosis and the macronucleus elongates and splits in half. Both new cells each obtain a copy of the micronucleus and macronucleus. Sexual reproduction involves conjugation, which involve two cells. After conjugation, the two cells divide, forming four new cells.

**Specialised Structures**

In some forms there are also body polykinetids, for instance, among the spirotrichs where they generally form bristles called *cirri*. More often body cilia are arranged in *mono-* and *dikinetids*, which respectively include one and two kinetosomes (basal bodies), each of which may support a cilium. These are arranged into rows called *kineties*, which run from the anterior to posterior of the cell. The body and oral kinetids make up the *infraciliature*, an organisation unique to the ciliates and important in their classification, and include various fibrils and microtubules involved in coordinating the cilia.

The infraciliature is one of the main component of the cell cortex. Another are the *alveoli*, small vesicles under the cell membrane that are packed against it to form a pellicle maintaining the cell's shape, which varies from flexible and contractile to rigid. Numerous mitochondria and extrusomes are also generally present. The presence of alveoli, the structure of the cilia, the form of mitosis and various other details indicate a close relationship between the ciliates, Apicomplexa, and dinoflagellates. These superficially dissimilar groups make up the alveolates.

## Fossil Record

Until recently, the oldest ciliate fossils known were tintinnids from the Ordovician Period. In 2007, Li *et al.* published a description of fossil ciliates from the Doushantuo Formation, about 580 million years ago, in the Ediacaran Period. These included two types of tintinnids and a possible ancestral suctorian.

## Apicomplexa

The Apicomplexa are a large group of protists, characterized by the presence of a unique organelle called an *apical complex* (see also apicoplast). They are unicellular, spore-forming, and exclusively parasites of animals. Motile structures such as flagella or pseudopods are absent except in certain gamete stages. This is a diverse group including organisms such as coccidia, gregarines, piroplasms, haemogregarines, and malarias; some diseases caused by apicomplexan organisms include:

- Babesiosis (*Babesia*)
- Malaria (*Plasmodium*)
- Coccidian diseases including:
  - Cryptosporidiosis (*Cryptosporidium parvum*)
  - Cyclosporiasis (*Cyclospora cayetanensis*)
  - Isosporiasis (*Isospora belli*)
  - Toxoplasmosis (*Toxoplasma gondii*)

Most members have a complex life-cycle, involving both asexual and sexual reproduction. Typically, a host is infected via an active invasion by the parasites (similar to entosis), which divide to produce *sporozoites* that enter its cells. Eventually, the cells burst, releasing *merozoites* which infect new cells. This may occur several times, until *gamonts* are produced, forming gametes that fuse to create new cysts. There are many variations on this basic pattern, however, and many Apicomplexa have more than one host.

The apical complex includes vesicles called rhoptries and micronemes, which open at the anterior of the cell. These secrete enzymes that allow the parasite to enter other cells. The tip is surrounded by a band of microtubules, called the polar ring, and among the Conoidasida there is also a funnel of rods called the conoid. Over the rest of the cell, except for a diminished mouth called the micropore, the membrane is supported by vesicles called alveoli, forming a semi-rigid pellicle.

The presence of alveoli and other traits place the Apicomplexa among a group called the alveolates. Several related flagellates, such as *Perkinsus* and *Colpodella* have structures similar to the polar ring and were formerly included here, but most appear to be closer relatives of the dinoflagellates. They are probably similar to the common ancestor of the two groups.

Another similarity is that apicomplexan cells contain a single plastid, called the apicoplast, surrounded by either 3 or four membranes. Its functions are thought to include tasks such as lipid synthesis, it appears to be necessary for survival. They are generally considered to share a common origin with the chloroplasts of dinoflagellates, and evidence generally points to an origin from red algae rather than green.

The Apicomplexa comprise the bulk of what used to be called the Sporozoa, a group for parasitic protozoans without flagella, pseudopods, or cilia. Most of the Apicomplexa are motile however. The other main lines were the Ascetosporea, the Myxozoa (now known to be derived from animals), and the Microsporidia (now known to be derived from fungi). Sometimes the name Sporozoa is taken as a synonym for the Apicomplexa, or occasionally as a subset.

**Disease Genomics**

As noted above, many of the apicomplexan parasites are important pathogens of human and domestic animals. In contrast to bacterial pathogens, these apicomplexan parasites are eukaryotes and share many metabolic pathways with their animal hosts. This fact makes therapeutic target development extremely difficult – a drug that harms an apicomplexan parasite is also likely to harm its human host. Currently there are no effective vaccines or treatments available for most diseases caused by these parasites.

Biomedical research on these parasites is challenging because it is often difficult, if not impossible, to maintain live parasite cultures in the laboratory and to genetically manipulate these organisms. In the recent years, several of the apicomplexan species have been selected for genome sequencing. The availability of genome sequences provides a new opportunity for scientists to learn more about the evolution and biochemical capacity of these parasite. A NIH-funded database, ApiDB.org, provides public access to currently available genomic data sets. One possible target for drugs is the plastid, and in fact existing drugs such as tetracyclines which are effective against apicomplexans seem to operate against the plastid.

Most apicomplexans have plastid genomes as well as nuclear ones, although *Cryptosporidium parvum* is an exception as it has lost its plastid genome.

## CHARACTERISTICS OF PROTISTS

Protists are eukaryotic organisms having true nuclei, membrane-enclosed organelles, "9+2" flagella and cilia. Mitosis and meiosis, occur in most species. Most are unicellular, some are colonial, and some are multicellular with tissues arranged in simple body plans. They are found in all moist environments. The free-living species are found in the seas, freshwater systems, and moist terrestrial habitats, and the symbiotic species are found in the body fluids, tissues and cells of the hosts. Almost all are aerobic, using mitochondria for cellular respiration, the anaerobic forms lack mitochondria and live in anaerobic environments or have a mutualistic relationship with respiring bacteria. The protists may be autotrophic, heterotrophic, or mixotrophic. Almost all have flagella or cilia (not homologous to prokaryotic flagella) at some time in the life cycle. The cilia and flagella are extensions of the cytoplasm. Cilia and flagella have the same basic structure; they differ only in that cilia are shorter and more numerous than are flagella.

Cell division in the Protista is varied and unique mitotic divisions occur in many groups. All can reproduce asexually; and some can reproduce sexually. Some form resistant cysts when stressed.

## THE ORIGIN OF EUKARYOTES

### A. The Antiquity of Eukaryotes

Precambrian acritarchs, dated 1.5 billion years old, are accepted as the oldest eukaryotic fossils known. They are similar in size and appearance to contemporary algal cysts. Eukaryotes evolved after $O_2$ accumulated in the primitive atmosphere.

### B. Models of Eukaryotic Origin

There are several models as to the origins of the Eukaryotic cell type:

Autogenous model = eukaryotic cells evolved by specialisation of internal membranes derived from prokaryotic plasma membranes. In this model most endomembranous structures are believed to have differentiated from invaginations of the prokaryotic plasma membrane. The double-membrane organelles (mitochondria and chloroplasts) may have evolved by secondary invagination or more complex membrane folding.

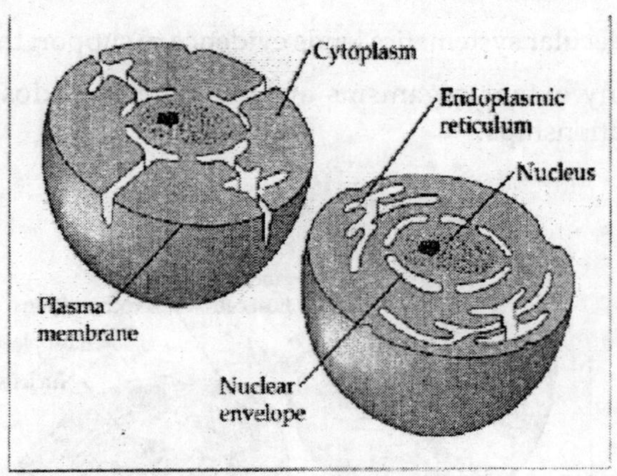


*Fig 6.1:* **The autogenous model**

Endosymbiotic model = certain prokaryotic species, called endosymbionts, lived within larger prokaryotes. This model focuses mainly on the origin of the mitochondria and chloroplasts. Chloroplasts are thought to have descended from endosymbiotic photosynthesising prokaryotes living in larger cells. Mitochondria are postulated to be descendants oi prokaryotic aerobic heterotrophs that may have been parasites or undigested prey of larger prokaryotes. The association progressed from parasitism or predation to mutualism.

Evidence for the endosymbiont model is that mitochondria and chloroplasts:

- are appropriate size to be descendants of eubacteria.
- have inner membranes containing several enzymes and transport systems similar to those on prokaryotic plasma membranes.
- replicate by splitting, as in prokaryotes.
- DNA is circular and not associated with histones or other proteins, as in prokaryotes.
- contain their own components for DNA transcription and translation into proteins.
- have ribosomes similar to prokaryotic ribosomes.
- molecular systematics lends evidence to support this theory.
- many extant organisms are involved in endosymbiotic relationships.

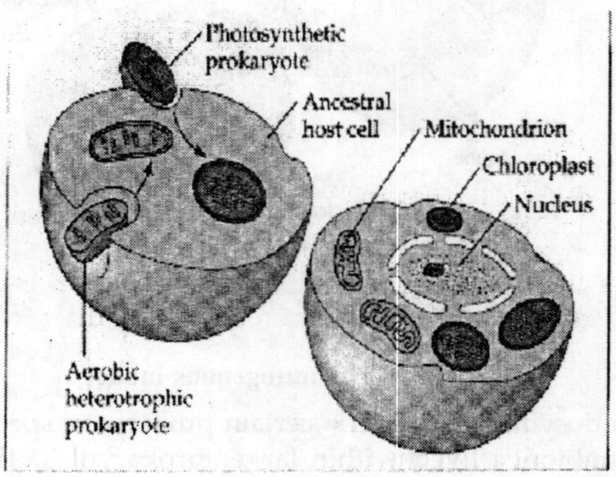


*Fig. 6.2:* **The endosymbiotic model**

Debate about which model of eukaryotic origin is most accurate continues. Evidence for the polyphyletic origin of eukaryotes has also been presented which may indicate that both models may be at least partially accurate.

## BOUNDARIES OF THE KINGDOM PROTISTA

In 1969, Robert H. Whittaker popularised the five kingdom taxonomic system and placed only unicellular eukaryotes in Protista. Now some multicellular algae and fungus-like organisms, previously classified with the plants and fungi, are placed in Kingdom Protista because they are believed to be more closely related to unicellular forms than to true plants or fungi. The taxonomy of protists is still in a state of flux. It is convenient to identify protozoa (animal-like protists), algae (plant-like protists) and the Slime Molds and Water Molds (fungus-like protists). This informal grouping does not reflect evolutionary relationships.

## PROTOZOA (Animal-like Protists)

This group more closely resembles the animals. The flagellate protozoans are believed to have been the ancestral form of the Kingdom Animalia. All protozoans are primarily heterotrophic, and usually obtain their food through some form of ingestion followed by intracellular digestion. As such, these organisms occupy a consumer role in the ecosystems they are located. A few are capable of alternating between a heterotrophic and autotrophic mode of nutrition, depending upon the resources available. Finally, some are internal or external parasites of animals. All protozoans are either unicellular or form small colonies of independent cells. The variations found within the group are mainly associated with the type of locomotion, cellular complexity and method of incorporating nutrients. The subdivision of this group into different phyla is based on how they feed and move. The general trend in the taxonomy is to distinguish between those animal-like protists that move by "cilia" the "Ciliophora", those protozoa that use flagella are called "Zoomastigophora" or pseudopodia to move are called "Rhizopoda", and those that don't move at all "Apicomplexa". One should not get too hung-up on the various taxonomic schemes, different people will place greater importance on different characteristics and this generates different schemes.

**Rhizopoda: Amoebas**

The amoeboid protists move by pseudopodia. These are not specific structures, but rather extensions of the cells, which are generated to allow movement along their course.

**Zoomastigophora: The Flagellates**

Flagellate protozoans have 1 to many flagella. The positions of the flagella vary from the apex to the side of the organism. Some of the flagellate forms are also colonial with the individual organisms joined on a stalk. The flagella may be used to propel the organism or to set up water currents to bring food to the organism. Species of *Trypanosoma* cause African sleeping sickness. This parasitic disease is spread by the bite of the tsetse fly.

**Foraminifera**

The amoeboid forms are often covered with a protective shell of $CaCO_3$. The cytoplasmic projections of pseudopodia are still used for motility or prey capture. These protozoa have porous, multi-chambered, calcium carbonate shells. They have cytoplasmic strands that extend through the shell's pores and function in swimming, feeding and shell formation. The foraminifera are exclusively marine. Most live in the sand or attach to algae and rocks; some are planktonic. The shells of the Foraminifera are an important component of sediments and sedimentary rocks.

**Actinopoda**

The members of this phylum also use slender pseudopodia for locomotion. these organisms differ from the Foraminaifera in the composition of the shells that surround them. In the Actinopoda the shells are made of silica, the same material in glass.

**Ciliophora: The Ciliates**

The ciliated protozoans, Ciliophora, are all unicellular. They represent some of the largest single celled organisms. The sizes of the cells range from a few microns in length to over 3 millimetres. Most exist as solitary cells in fresh water. The outer covering, or pellicle, is generally covered with cilia that beat in unison to propel the organism with a spinning motion. These Cilia may be dispersed over surface, or clustered in fewer rows or tufts. Some ciliates move on leg-like cirri (many cilia bonded together) (eg. *Euplotes* sp.), others have rows of tightly packed cilia that function together as locomotor membranes (for example, *Stentor* sp.)

### Apicomplexa: The Sporozoans

These non-motile protozoans are spore forming, unicellular parasites of higher animals. They are unique due to a complex arrangement of organelles at one end of the cell.

The life cycles of these parasites are intricate with both sexual and asexual reproduction occurring; often requiring two or more different host species. For example, several species of *Plasmodium* cause malaria. This is a potentially fatal and relatively common tropical disease resulting in at least one million deaths each year. Below is the life cycle of *Plasmodium* sp.

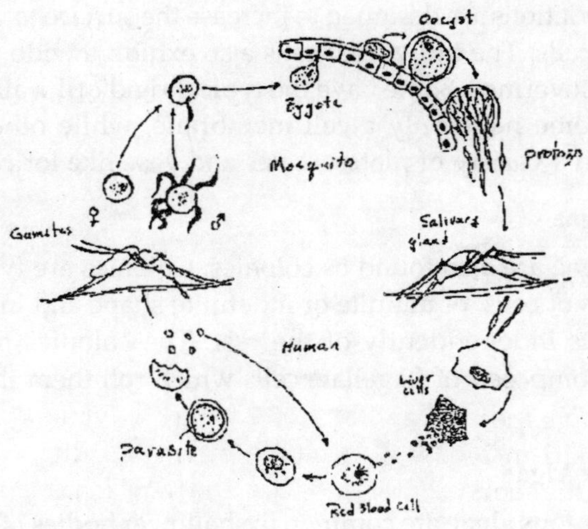


*Fig. 6.3:* Life cycle of *Plasmodium* sp.

## THE PLANT-LIKE PROTISTA (The Algae)

The greatest cellular and morphological diversity in the kingdom occurs within the algae. While the majority of the group are unicellular, there are also species which are colonial, filamentous, coenocytic and multicellular.

Algal protists are aquatic organisms which have chiorophyll a (like cyanobacteria and plants). They differ from other photosynthetic organisms in that they also have accessory pigments such as carotenoids, xanthophylls, phycobillins, and other forms of chlorophyll.

## Morphological Diversity of the Algae

In this section we will examine the various morphologies found in the algae. We will not survey each of the different divisions (Phyla) as your textbook does. Instead we will look at how these various morphologies have adapted these organisms to survive in the aquatic habitat.

### Unicellular Algae

The unicellular algae are all sizes and shapes. They range from small spherical cells to large irregular shaped cells. Most of the shape variations are designed to increase the surface to volume ratio of the cells. The individual cells also exhibit a wide variety of different coverings. Some have the typical rigid cell wall found in plants. Some have only a cell membrane, while others are covered with a variety of plates, scales and vase like loricae.

### Colonial Algae

The algae are also found as colonies. Colonies are typically aggregations of cells, of definite or indefinite shape and in which each cell acts independently of the rest. The colonies may be floating or composed of flagellate cells which roll them through the water.

### Filamentous Algae

Filamentous algae are common in shallower bodies of water. The filaments can be free floating or more commonly, attached to the bottom by a modified cell termed a holdfast. As with the colonial forms, except for the holdfast, the cells of the filaments are all alike and function independently of each other. A few of the apparently filamentous algae lack any cross walls along the length of the filament. The organism is then a continuous protoplasmic mass controlled by several nuclei. This is termed a coenocytic filament. In the larger Rhodophyta or red algae, the filaments are combined to form large macroscopic individuals, sometimes reaching lengths of up to 1 or more metres.

**Seaweed**

This is a common name for all the large complex multicellular algae. These organisms belong to several phyla including the Brown algae (Phaeophyta), the Red algae (Rhodophyta) and some Green algae (Chlorophyta). These seaweeds have the most complex multicellular anatomy of any of the algae. Some even have tissues and organs that resemble those of the higher land plants. However, these seaweeds are more closely related to the unicellular algae then they are to the land plants, and their anatomical complexity evolved independently. The term thallus (thalli *pl.*) is used to describe the seaweed body form. A typical seaweed has a root like holdfast which anchors the plant to the substrate, a stem like stipe, and a leaf like blade. The blades provide most of the photosynthetic surface for the algae.

**Evolutionary Adaptations of Seaweed**

Many seaweeds are large, multicellular marine algae which are found in the intertidal and subtidal zones of coastal waters. The habitat of seaweeds, particularly the intertidal zone, poses several challenges to the survival of these organisms. Firstly the movement of the water due to wave action and winds produces a physically active habitat. Secondly the tidal rhythms result in the seaweeds being alternately covered by seawater and exposed to direct sunlight and the drying conditions of the air. Seaweeds have evolved several unique structural and biochemical adaptations to survive the conditions of their habitats.

Structural adaptations found in seaweeds are a result of their complex multicellular anatomy. Some forms have differentiated tissues and organs analogous to those of plants. The body of a seaweed is called a thallus. It is plant-like in appearance but has no true roods, stems, or leaves. A thallus consists of a root-like holdfast (maintains position), a stem-like stipe (supports the blades), and leaf-like blades (large surfaces for photosynthesis). Floats which help suspend blades near the water surface are present in some brown algae.

Biochemical adaptations in some red and brown algae reinforce the anatomical adaptations and enhance survival. Cellulose cell walls also contain gel-forming polysaccharides (algin in brown algae; carageenan in red algae) which cushion the thalli against wave action and prevent desiccation during low tide. Some red algae retard grazing by marine invertebrates by incorporating large amounts of calcium carbonate into their cell walls. Seaweeds are used by humans in a variety of ways: food, nutrient supplements, additives, lubricants, and microbiological culture media.

**Reproduction in the Plant-like Protista**

Asexual reproduction occurs most frequently in the algal divisions. Some algae never reproduce sexually. Most use sexual reproduction once a year and all the rest of the algal biomass is generated through one form or another of asexual reproduction. The following types of asexual reproduction occur in the algae.

**(a) Cell division or binary fission**

- one of the most common types
- occurs daily and sometimes as fast as every 4h
- involves mitosis followed by cytokinesis

**(b) Fragmentation**

- found in colonial or filamentous algae
- usually involves an accidental break-up of the original organism, followed by a regeneration of the fragments through cell growth and enlargement

**(c) Daughter colony formation**

- one or more cells of the colony divides and produces an exact replica of the parent colony, with exactly the same number of cells.
- rare

**(d) Sporulation**

- most common and productive form of asexual reproduction in the algae

- found in all morphological types
- begins with mitosis to produce 2 or more nuclei in a cell (sporangium)
- the cytoplasm collects around each of the nuclei form 2 or more cells (spores) inside the parent cell wall
- the new spores are released and grow into new algae.

The types of sexual reproduction found in the algae are as varied as asexual reproduction. Variations occur in the type of gametes, the type of gametangia, the site of fertilisation, the relative importance of each generation and the fate of the zygote.

The types of gametes can be summarised by the following terms:

1. Isogamy = the male and female gametes are morphologically indistinguishable
2. Anisogamy = the male and female gametes differ in size or morphology
3. Oogamy = a flagellated male gamete (sperm) fertilises a nonmotile female gamete (egg)

Below is one of the most frequent types of life cycles found in the green algae (Fig. 6.4).

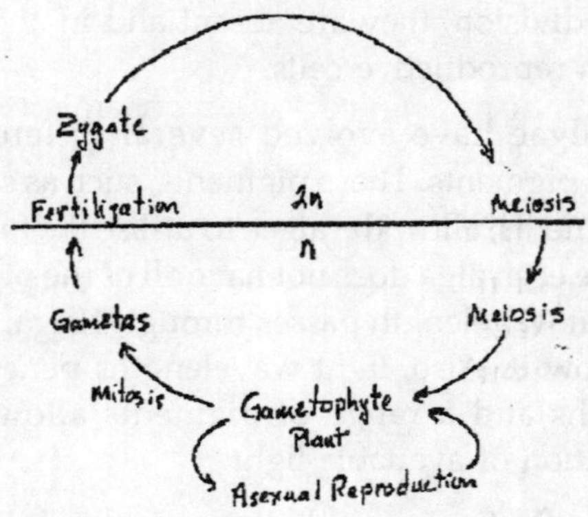


***Fig 6.4:*** **Types of life cycles of green algae**

**Environmental Adaptations of the Algae**

The algae are all, at some point, autotrophic organisms. They utilise radiant energy from the sun as their direct energy source, and carbon from $CO_2$ to produce their organic carbon molecules. As autotrophic organisms or primary producers, they occupy the base of aquatic food chains. In this role, the algae are essential to the survival of the entire aquatic community.

To ensure they will receive adequate light for photosynthesis, algae have evolved several different adaptations. Since the light is only in the upper waters, the algae must stay up in this photic zone. If they sink too rapidly below this zone, they will die. If they sink slowly, they may either be brought back up to the surface waters through currents or survive on the bottom because of various dormancy methods. To reduce sinking rates, the algae have developed ways of increasing their surface:volume (S:V) ratios. A large surface area creates a greater friction between the water and the cell surfaces. A relatively smaller volume reduces the pull generated by the denser cytoplasm. Such mechanisms include smaller size of cells, surface projections such as spines and production of lighter compounds such as lipids as food storage products. Secretion of a low density mucilage also retards the sinking rate. Another way in which the algae are able to move within the photic zone is by swimming in still waters with flagella. Almost every algal division has flagellate cells although, in 1 division, they are absent and in another they are only present in reproductive cells.

Finally, algae have evolved several different accessory photosynthetic pigments. These pigments, such as carotenoid and phycobilin pigments, allow the algae to utilise the full light energy spectrum. Since each alga does not have all of the pigments, when light of a certain wavelength passes through 1 alga, it can be used by an alga below it. Also, light wavelengths penetrate water to different depths and a range of pigments allows for a more efficient utilisation of available light.

These modifications may also increase the ability of to obtain more nutrients and to avoid some of the natural predators (Herbivores).

## FUNGAL-LIKE PROTISTA

This is the smallest of the three groups of protists. These organisms superficially resemble fungi, however they are not believed to have given rise to the true fungi. The origin of the true fungi that we will study next is still a mystery.

These organisms, like the protozoans, are all heterotrophic. They differ from the protozoans since the vast majority do not ingest their food prior to (extracellular digestion) chemical processing. These organisms occupy a decomposer role in the ecosystem. Along with the more advanced fungi and bacteria, they are essential for restoring inorganic nutrients back to the environment, and for preventing the accumulation of excess remains of dead organisms.

Variation within this group is based primarily upon differences in cellular organisation. Some are unicellular, some coenocytic blobs while still others are coenocytic hyphae.

The two small groups of fungal-like Protista, the cellular and acellular slime molds behave like the amoeboid protozoans. They move along the substrate engulfing food with pseudopodia and then digesting it in food vacuoles. The largest group, Oomycota, behave more as fungi. The organisms adhere to the surface or grow inside plants, animals, the remains of plants and animals or on processed organic material. From this position, the organisms release exoenzymes which break down food material into small organic molecules which can then be transported directly across the cell membranes. Often the organisms, which are coenocytic hyphae, produce small hyphal branches that extend directly into the cells of the host organism. If the host is a plant, they may digest and absorb the entire cell contents, leaving only the cell wall as an empty skeleton.

As with the protozoan parasites, the Oomycota can also be very host specific. This means they will be able to utilise only 1 or a few hosts as food.

### Reproduction in the fungal-like Protista

Sporulation and cell division are the two major forms of asexual reproduction in this group. The slime molds increase asexually through cell division, while the Oomycota use sporulation.

Sexual reproduction in these organisms is again limited to 1 or a few times during a year. The life cycles associated with the sexual reproduction are less varied than in the algae.

## CHLOROPHYTA

### Scientific Classification

| | | |
|---|---|---|
| Domain | : | Eukarya |
| Kingdom | : | Plantae |
| Division | : | Chlorophyta |

### Classes

Bryopsidophyceae

Chlorophyceae

Pedinophyceae

Pleurastrophyceae

Prasinophyceae

Trebouxiophyceae

Ulvophyceae

Chlorophyta, a division of green algae, includes about 7000 species f mostly aquatic photosynthetic eukaryotic organisms. Like the land plants (bryophytes and tracheophytes), green algae contain chlorophylls *a* and *b*, and store food as starch n their plastids. They are related to the Charophyta and Embryophyta (land plants), together making up the Viridiplantae.

The division contains both unicellular and multicellular species. While most species live in freshwater habitats and a large number in marine habitats, other species are adapted to a wide range of environments. Watermelon snow, or *Chlamydomonas nivalis*, of the class Chlorophyceae, lives on summer alpine snowfields. Others live attached to rocks or woody parts of trees. Some lichens are symbiotic relationships with fungi and a green alga. Members of the Chlorophyta also form symbiotic relationships with protozoa, sponges and cnidarians. Some are flagellated and these have an advantage of motility. Some conduct sexual reproduction which is oogamy or isogamy.

**Classes**

- Class Bryopsidophyceae Bessey
- Class Chlorophyceae Wille
- Class Pedinophyceae Moestrup
- Class Pleurastrophyceae Mattox & K. D. Stewart
- Class Prasinophyceae T.A. Chr. ex Ø. Moestrup & J. Throndsen
- Class Trebouxiophyceae T. Friedl
- Class Ulvophyceae K.R. Mattox & K.D. Stewart
- Class Caryopoceae Jerry

Classification according to Hoek, Mann and Jahns 1995.[4]

- *Prasinophyceae*
- *Chlorophyceae*
- *Ulvophyceae*
- *Cladophorophyceae*
- *Bryopsipophycese*
- *Dasycladophyceae*
- *Trentepoliophyceae*
- *Pleurastrophyceae* (Pleurastrales and Prasiolales)
- *Klebsormidiophyceae*
- *Zygnematophyceae*
- *Charophyceae*

Classification according to Bold and Wynne (Introduction to the Algae, Second Edition, Prentice Hall NJ)

- *Volvocales*
- *Tetrasporales*
- *Chlorococcales*
- *Chlorosarcinales*

- *Ulotrichales*
- *Sphaeropleales*
- *Chaetophorales*
- *Trentepohliales*
- *Oedogoniales*
- *Ulvales*
- *Cladophorales*
- *Acrosiphoniales*
- *Caulerpales*
- *Siphonocladales*
- *Dasycladales*

## FLAGELLATE

Flagellates are cells with one or more whip-like organelles called flagella. Some cells in animals may be flagellate, for instance the spermatozoa of most phyla. Higher plants and fungi do not produce flagellate cells, but the closely related green algae and chytrids do. Many protists take the form of single-celled flagellates.

### Form and behaviour

Flagellates are protozoans (animal-like protists). Eukaryotic flagella are supported by microtubules in a characteristic arrangement, with nine fused pairs surrounding two central singlets. These arise from a basal body or kinetosome, with microtubule roots that are an important part of the cell's brain. In some, for instance, they support a cytostome or mouth, where food is ingested. The flagella often support hairs, called mastigonemes, or contain rods. Their ultrastructure plays an important role in classifying eukaryotes.

In protists and microscopic animals, flagella are generally used for propulsion. They may also be used to create a current that brings in food. In most things, one or more flagella are located at or near the anterior of the cell eg Euglena. Often there is one directed forwards and one trailing behind. Among animals, fungi, and Choanozoa, which make up a group called the opisthokonts, there is a single posterior flagellum. They are from the phylum Mastigophora. They can cause diseases and they can make their own food. For example, Trypanosome which causes the African sleeping sickness.

Originally, the flagellated protozoa were treated as a single class of the phylum Mastigophora. This was divided into the Phytomastigina or phytoflagellates, which have chloroplasts or are closely related to such forms, and the Zoomastigina or zooflagellates, which do not. Most phytoflagellates were given a separate classification by botanists, treating them in several divisions of algae.

This scheme has generally been abandoned or is retained only for convenience. However, the relationships among the flagellates are still mostly unknown, and their higher classification is confused. Some argue that the Linnaean ranks are not appropriate for such a diverse set of organisms.

Phytoflagellates are found in most groups of algae. Both the green algae and heterokonts include a variety of flagellates in addition to non-motile and multicellular forms. The dinoflagellates, cryptomonads, haptophytes, and euglenids are almost entirely single-celled flagellates.

Many of the other flagellates make up what are called the excavate taxa. These include the euglenids and a number of important parasites, such as trypanosomes and *Giardia*. The excavates generally show similarities in the structure of their flagella and typically have a cytostome. However, they may be a paraphyletic group, and in particular may have been ancestral to most or all other eukaryotes.

Other notable groups including flagellates are the Cercozoa, alveolates (including dinoflagellates), ebriids, and Apusozoa.

## FLAGELLUM

A flagellum (Plural: flagella) is a tail-like structure that projects from the cell body of certain prokaryotic and eukaryotic cells, and it functions in locomotion. An example of a eukaryotic flagellated cell is the sperm cell, which uses its flagellum to propel itself toward and through the female reproductive tract. An example of a flagellated bacterium is the ulcer-causing *Helicobacter pylori,* which uses its multiple flagella to propel itself through the mucus lining to reach the stomach epithelium. Prokaryotic and eukaryotic flagella have some notable differences, such as protein composition, structure, and mechanism of propulsion. Flagella are structurally identical to eukaryotic cilia, although distinctions are sometimes made according to function and/or length. Flagella are cellular *structures,* not organelles.

The word *flagellum* comes from the Latin for whip.

**Types**

Three quite distinct types of flagella have so far been distinguished; bacterial, archaeal and eukaryotic.

The main differences among these three types are summarized below:

- *Bacterial flagella* are helical filaments that rotate like screws. They provide two of several kinds of bacterial motility.
- *Archaeal flagella* are superficially similar to bacterial flagella, but are different in many details and considered non-homologous.
- *Eukaryotic flagella* - those of animal, plant, and protist cells - are complex cellular projections that lash back and forth.

Sometimes eukaryotic flagella are called *cilia* or *undulipodia* to emphasize their distinctiveness.

Examples of bacterial flagella arrangement schemes. A-Monotrichous; B-Lophotrichous; C-Amphitrichous; D-Peritrichous.

The bacterial flagellum is made up of the protein flagellin. Its shape is a 20 nanometer-thick hollow tube. It is helical and has a sharp bend just outside the outer membrane; this "hook" allows the helix to point directly away from the cell. A shaft runs between the hook and the basal body, passing through protein rings in the cell's membrane that act as bearings. Gram-positive organisms have 2 of these basal body rings, one in the peptidoglycan layer and one in the plasma membrane. Gram-negative organisms have 4 such rings: the L ring associates with the lipopolysaccharides, the P ring associates with peptidoglycan layer, the M ring is embedded in the plasma membrane, and the S ring is directly attached to the plasma membrane. The filament ends with a capping protein.

The bacterial flagellum is driven by a rotary engine made up of protein (Mot complex), located at the flagellum's anchor point on the inner cell membrane. The engine is powered by proton motive force, i.e., by the flow of protons (hydrogen ions) across the bacterial cell membrane due to a concentration gradient set up by the cell's metabolism (*in Vibrio* species there are two kinds of flagella, lateral and polar, and some are driven by a sodium ion pump rather than a proton pump . The rotor transports protons across the membrane, and is turned in the process. The rotor alone can operate at 6,000 to 17,000 rpm, but with the flagellar filament attached usually only reaches 200 to 1000 rpm.

Flagella do not rotate at a constant speed but instead can increase or decrease their rotational speed in relation to the strength of the proton motive force. Flagellar rotation can move bacteria through liquid media at speeds of up to 60 cell lengths/ second . Although this is only about 0.00017 km/h, when comparing this speed with that of higher organisms in terms of number of lengths moved per second, it is extremely fast. The fastest land animal, the cheetah, moves at a maximum rate of about 110 km/h, but this represents only about 25 body lengths/ sec. Thus, when size is accounted for, prokaryotic cells swimming at 50-60 lengths/sec are actually much faster than larger organisms.

The components of the bacterial flagellum are capable of self-assembly without the aid of enzymes or other factors. Both the basal body and the filament have a hollow core, through which the component proteins of the flagellum are able to move into their respective positions. During assembly, protein components are added at the flagellar tip rather than at the base.

The basal body has several traits in common with some types of secretory pores, such as the hollow rod-like "plug" in their centres extending out through the plasma membrane. Given the structural similarities, it was thought that bacterial flagella may have evolved from such pores; however, it is now known that these pores are derived from flagella.

**Flagella Arrangement Schemes**

Different species of bacteria have different numbers and arrangements of flagella. Monotrichous bacteria have a single flagellum (e.g., *Vibrio cholerae*). Lophotrichous bacteria have multiple flagella located at the same spot on the bacteria's surfaces which act in concert to drive the bacteria in a single direction. In many cases, the bases of multiple flagella are surrounded a specialized region of the cell membrane; the so-called *polar membrane*. Amphitrichous bacteria have a single flagellum on each of two opposite ends (only one flagellum operates at a time, allowing the bacteria to reverse course rapidly by switching which flagellum is active). Peritrichous bacteria have flagella projecting in all directions (e.g., *Escherichia coli*).

In some bacteria, such as the larger forms of *Selenomonas*, the individual flagella are organized outside the cell body, helically twining about each other to form a thick structure called a "fascicle". Other bacteria, such as Spirochetes, have a specialized type of flagellum called an "axial filament" that is located in the periplasmic space, the rotation of which causes the entire bacterium to move forward in a corkscrew-like motion.

Counterclockwise rotation of monotrichous polar flagella thrust the cell forward with the flagella trailing behind. Periodically, the direction of rotation is briefly reversed, causing what is known as a "tumble" in which the cell seems to thrash about in place. This results in the reorientation of the cell. When moving in a favorable direction, "tumbles" are unlikely; however, when the cell's direction of motion is unfavorable (e.g., away from a chemical attractant), a tumble may occur, with the chance that the cell will be thus reoriented in the correct direction.

In some *Vibrio* (particularly *Vibrio parahemolyticus* and related proteobacteria such as *Aeromonas*, two flagellar systems co-exist, using different sets of genes and different ion gradients for energy. The polar flagella are constitutively expressed and provide motility in bulk fluid, while the lateral flagella are expressed when the polar flagella meets too much resistance to turn These provide swarming motility on surfaces or in viscous fluids.

**Archaeal**

The archaeal flagellum is superficially similar to the bacterial (or eubacterial) flagellum; in the 1980s they were thought to be homologous on the basis of gross morphology and behaviour. Both flagella consist of filaments extending outside of the cell, and rotate to propel the cell.

However, discoveries in the 1990s revealed numerous detailed differences between the archaeal and bacterial flagella; these include:

- Bacterial flagella are motorized by a flow of $H^+$ ions (or occasionally $Na^+$ ions); archaeal flagella are almost certainly powered by ATP. The torque-generating motor that powers rotation of the archaeal flagellum has not been identified.
- While bacterial cells often have many flagellar filaments, each of which rotates independently, the archaeal flagellum is composed of a bundle of many filaments that rotate as a single assembly.
- Bacterial flagella grow by the addition of flagellin subunits at the tip; archaeal flagella grow by the addition of subunits to the base.
- Bacterial flagella are thicker than archaeal flagella, and the bacterial filament has a large enough hollow "tube" inside that the flagellin subunits can flow up the inside of the filament and get added at the tip; the archaeal flagellum is too thin to allow this.
- Many components of bacterial flagella share sequence similarity to components of the type III secretion systems, but the components of bacterial and archaeal flagella share no sequence similarity. Instead, some components of archaeal flagella share sequence and morphological

similarity with components of type IV pili, which are assembled through the action of type II secretion systems (the nomenclature of pili and protein secretion systems is not consistent).

These differences mean that the bacterial and archaeal flagella are a classic case of biological analogy, or convergent evolution, rather than homology. However, in comparison to the decades of well-publicized study of bacterial flagella (e.g. by Berg), archaeal flagella have only recently begun to get serious scientific attention. Therefore, many assume erroneously that there is only one basic kind of prokaryotic flagellum, and that archaeal flagella are homologous to it. For example, Cavalier-Smith (2002 is aware of the differences between archaeal and bacterial flagellins, but retains the misconception that the basal bodies are homologous.

**Eukaryotic**

The eukaryotic flagellum is completely different from the prokaryote flagellum in both structure and evolutionary origin. The only shared characteristics among bacterial, archaeal, and eukaryotic flagella are their superficial appearance; they are intracellular extensions used in creating movement. Along with cilia, flagella make up a group of organelles known as undulipodia.

**Structure**

A eukaryotic flagellum is a bundle of nine fused pairs of microtubule *doublets* surrounding two central single microtubules. The so-called "9+2" structure is characteristic of the core of the eukaryotic flagellum called an *axoneme*. At the base of a eukaryotic flagellum is a basal body, "blepharoplast" or kinetosome, which is the microtubule organizing center (MTOC) for flagellar microtubules and is about 500 nanometers long. Basal bodies are structurally identical to centrioles. The flagellum is encased within the cell's plasma membrane, so that the interior of the flagellum is accessible to the cell's cytoplasm.

Each of the outer 9 doublet microtubules extends a pair of dynein arms (an "inner" and an "outer" arm) to the adjacent microtubule; these dynein arms are responsible for flagellar beating, as the force produced by the arms causes the microtubule doublets to slide against each other and the flagellum as a whole to bend. These dynein arms produce force through ATP hydrolysis. The flagellar axoneme also contains radial spokes, polypeptide complexes extending from each of the outer 9 microtubule doublets towards the central pair, with the "head" of the spoke facing inwards. The radial spoke is thought to be involved in the regulation of flagellar motion, although its exact function and method of action are not yet understood.

### Flagella vs Cilia

Though eukaryotic flagella and cilia are ultrastructurally identical, the beating pattern of the two organelles can be different. In the case of flagella (e.g. the tail of a sperm) the motion is propeller-like. In contrast, beating of cilia consists of coordinated back-and-forth cycling of many cilia on the cell surface. Thus, motile flagella serve for the propulsion of single cells (e.g. swimming of protozoa and spermatozoa), and cilia for the transport of fluids (e.g. transport of mucus by stationary ciliated cells in the trachea). However, cilia are also used for locomotion (through liquids) in organisms such as *Paramecium*.

### Intraflagellar Transport

Intraflagellar transport (IFT), the process by which axonemal subunits, transmembrane receptors, and other proteins are moved up and down the length of the flagellum, is essential for proper functioning of the flagellum, in both motility and signal transduction.

For information on biologists' ideas about how the various flagella may have evolved, see evolution of flagella.

### Irreducible Complexity

In his 1996 book *Darwin's Black Box*, intelligent design proponent Michael Behe cited the bacterial flagellum as an example of an irreducibly complex structure that could not have evolved through naturalistic means. Behe argued that the flagellum becomes useless if any one of its constituent parts is removed, and thus could not have arisen through numerous, successive, slight modifications; therefore, it is hopelessly improbable that the proteins making up the flagellar motor could have come together all at once, by chance.

While Behe discussed the immune system and the blood clotting cascade in greater detail, the bacterial flagellum has become a "poster child" for intelligent design proponents and other creationists. It is one of two identified rotary structures found in nature (the other being ATP synthase) and it is billions of years older than Behe's other two examples, which exist in many homologous forms, simplifying the explanation of their origin.

Evolutionary pathways have since been proposed for the bacterial flagellum. In addition, the Type III secretory system, a molecular syringe which bacteria use to inject toxins into other cells, appears to be a simplified sub-set of the bacterial flagellum's components, meaning that it is much less likely to be irreducibly complex. Behe's arguments have been examined and rejected by the scientific community at large. Exaptation explains how systems with multiple parts can evolve through natural means.

**Evolution of Flagella**

The evolution of flagella is of great interest to biologists because the three known varieties of flagella (eukaryotic, bacterial, and archaebacterial) each represent an extremely sophisticated cellular structure that requires the interaction of many different and finely-tuned systems to function correctly.

**The Eukaryotic Flagellum**

There are two competing groups of models for the evolutionary origin of the eukaryotic flagellum (referred to as cilium below to distinguish it from its bacterial counterpart).

**Symbiotic/Endosymbiotic/Exogenous Models**

These models argue some version of the idea that the cilium evolved from a symbiotic spirochete that attached to a primitive eukaryote or archaebacterium (archaea). The modern version of the hypothesis was first proposed by Lynn Margulis (as Sagan (1967): Margulis was the first wife of the late Carl Sagan). The hypothesis, though very well publicized, was never widely accepted by the experts, in contrast to Margulis' arguments for the symbiotic origin of mitochondria and chloroplasts.

The primary point in favor of the symbiotic hypothesis is that there are eukaryotes that use symbiotic spirochetes as their motility organelles (some parabasalids inside termite guts, such as *Mixotricha* and *Trichonympha*). While this is an example of co-option and the flexibility of biological systems, none of the proposed homologies that have been reported between cilia and spirochetes have stood up to further scrutiny. The homology of tubulin to the bacterial replication/cytoskeletal protein FtsZ is a major argument against Margulis, as FtsZ is apparently found native in archaea, providing an endogenous ancestor to tubulin (as opposed to Margulis' hypothesis, that an archaea acquired tubulin from a symbiotic spirochete).

At present the symbiotic hypothesis for the origin of cilia seems to be limited to Margulis and a few of her associates. Margulis is, though, still strongly promoting and publishing a revised version of her hypothesis (Margulis' 1998 book *Symbiotic planet: a new look at evolution* has some frank autobiographical comments about her support of the symbiotic hypothesis for the origin of the cilium).

**Endogenous/Autogenous/Direct Filiation Models**

Contrasting with the symbiotic models, these models argue that cilia developed from pre-existing components of the eukaryotic cytoskeleton (which has tubulin, dynein, and nexin—also used for other functions) as an extension of the mitotic spindle apparatus. The connection can still be seen, first in the various early-branching single-celled eukaryotes that have a microtubule basal body, where microtubules on one end form a spindle-like cone around the nucleus, while microtubules on the other end point away from the cell and form the cilium. A further connection is that the centriole, involved in the formation of the mitotic spindle in many (but not all) eukaryotes, is homologous to the cilium, and in many cases *is* the basal body from which the cilium grows.

An apparent intermediate stage between spindle and cilium would be a non-swimming appendage made of microtubules with a selectable function like increasing surface area, helping the protozoan to remain suspended in water, increasing the chances of bumping into bacteria to eat, or serving as a stalk attaching the cell to a solid substrate.

Regarding the origin of the individual protein components, an interesting paper on the evolution of dyneins shows that the more complex protein family of ciliary dynein has an apparent ancestor in a simpler cytoplasmic dynein (which itself has evolved from the AAA protein family that occurs widely in all archea, bacteria and eukaryotes). Long-standing suspicions that tubulin was homologous to FtsZ (based on very weak sequence similarity and some behavioural similarities) were confirmed in 1998 by the independent resolution of the 3-dimensional structures of the two proteins.

**The Bacterial Flagellum**

An approach to the evolutionary origin of the bacterial flagellum is suggested by the fact that a subset of flagellar components can function as a Type III transport system.

Admittedly, all currently known nonflagellar Type III transport systems are for injecting toxin into eukaryotic cells, and are therefore presumably descended from the flagellum, which is likely older than eukaryotes. For example, the bubonic plague bacterium *Yersinia pestis* has an organelle assembly very similar to a complex flagellum except that it functions as a needle to inject toxins into host cells.

However, the Type III transport system still undergirds the hypothesis that the flagellum did not have to come about all at once, as a subset of components has a selectable function. That all known nonflagellar Type III transport systems are disease mechanisms is not shocking, because the Type III secretion system was only discovered in 1994 and scientific study of eubacteria is significantly biased towards disease-causing organisms. This provides another case of co-option, where a motility organelle has evolved into a "complex weapon for close combat."

**The Archaeal Flagellum**

The recently elucidated archaeal flagellum is analogous, not homologous, to the bacterial one. In addition to no sequence similarity being detected between the genes of the two systems, the archaeal flagellum appears to grow at the base rather than the tip, and is about 15 nanometers (nm) in diameter rather than

20. Sequence comparison indicates that the archaeal flagellum is homologous to Type IV pili[3] (pili are filamentous structures outside the cell). Interestingly, some Type IV pili can retract. Pilus retraction provides the driving force for a different form of bacterial motility called "twitching" or "social gliding" which allows bacterial cells to crawl along a surface. Thus Type IV pili can, in different bacteria, promote either swimming or crawling. Type IV pili are assembled through the Type II transport system. So far, no species of bacteria is known to use its Type IV pili for both swimming and crawling.

Testable outlines exist for the origin of each of the three motility systems, and avenues for further research are clear; for prokaryotes, these avenues include the study of secretion systems in free-living, nonvirulent prokaryotes. In eukaryotes, the mechanisms of both mitosis and cilial construction, including the key role of the centriole, need to be much better understood. A detailed survey of the various nonmotile appendages found in eukaryotes is also necessary. Finally, the study of the origin of all of these systems would benefit greatly from a resolution of the questions surrounding deep phylogeny—what are the most deeply branching organisms in each domain, and what are the interrelationships between the domains.

# Chapter–7

# Biosynthesis of Cellulose

## INTRODUCTION

The most dominant polysaccharide of the cell wall is cellulose. The universal distribution of this natural polymer among prokaryotic and eukaryotic organisms attests to its ancient evolutionary history. Not only is cellulose found among photosynthetic and protistan cells, it is present in animals such as the Ascidians. Furthermore, levels of elevated cellulose synthesis have been suggested in humans with the disease scleroderma.

The algae have been prominent organisms of study among eukaryotic organisms because of their great diversity of structure and cellular organisation. Chloroplast morphology, organisation of the mitotic apparatus, cell wall structure and composition, flagellar apparatus and reproduction have provided a wealth of information on algal phylogeny; however, very few studies have concentrated on evolutionary and phylogenetic aspects of cell walls, let alone cellulose, mainly because the cellulose synthases had never been observed or isolated.

In 1976, the first successful application of freeze fracture demonstrated the structure of a cellulose synthase complex in Oocystis apiculata.

These membrane associated structures, called terminal synthesizing complexes (=TCs), were found at the growing tip of microfibril impressions on the E-fracture face of the plasma membrane. Earlier, Roelofsen (1958) had predicted that an organized terminal enzyme complex would be found; howver, the shape and geometry could not be predicted at that time.

In 1964, Preston proposed the ordered granule hypothesis for the cellulose synthase complex. This study was based on observations of remnants of organized particle subunits associated with the innermost wall of Chaetomorpha. During this time, the freeze fracture technique was becoming widely used, and organized particle complexes were found in the plasma membranes, particularly abundant in yeasts. Thus, a logical extension of the possibility of such an organisation could be made for the cellulose synthesizing complex. Interestingly, TCs were not observed in cells which had been chemically fixed or treated with glycerol or cryoprotectants. The breakthrough in finding TCs came when Brown and Montezinos demonstrated thatrapid direct freezing of living cells yielded organized particle structures associated with the tips of microfibrils.

Since 1976, TCs have been found in more than 14 algal genera, and presently, a distinct pattern of TC structure is beginning to emerge which provides some insight into the substantial diversity of cellulose microfibril synthesis among the algae. In this presentation, the fundamental TC diversity among the algae will be described. Because TC variation is the greatest among the algae, it also provides hints at the relationship between TC organisation and microfibril shape, molecular weight of the cellulose, and crystallization. Phylogenetic relationships based on TC structure can be correlated with other structural and biochemical evidence. This presentation will conclude with a proposed evolutionary history of cellulose biogenesis.

## TERMINAL COMPLEX DIVERSITY

So far, only two basic forms of TCs have been found among eukaryotic cells. The linear TC was first discovered in Oocystis and is present among most members of theUlvophyceae.

Unlike that in the corn root, the rosette TC found in Micrasterias frequently is organized in ordered arrays, especially during secondary wall formation. Furthermore, the rosette subunits have been shown to span both layers of the bimolecular leaflet. Since these first reports, rosette TC's have been found in a variety of organisms, ranging from the land plants to Chara (McLean andJuniper, 1986) and Nitella.

Interestingly, only the rosette TC has been found among the vascular plants. Thus, algal ancestors with rosette TCs have assumed added importance with respect to understanding the evolution of land plants.

For a more detailed elaboration of the distribution of TC's among eukaryotic cells, consult the report of Brown. Since this publication, TCs have been found in other organisms and will briefly described. In 1987, Hotchkiss and Brown described a solitary rosette TC in Nitella translucens. This TC is virtually indistinguishable from that of land plants, in addition, a solitary-rosette TC has been observed in Chara.

Only in the Zygnematales has an ordered consolidation of TC's been found, and among one member, Mougeotia, eTCs are exclusively solitary. Thus, the consolidation of rosette TCs appears to have been a more recent event. When wall composition is taken into consideration, the evidence strongly supports that the Charophyceae is the phylogenetic line which may have given rise to the vascular plants.

Another interesting and different TC structure recently was found in the xanthophycean genus, Vaucheria. Overall, the TC is linear, but the subunit arrangement within the TC is in the form of unique diagonal rows.

The relationship between TC geometry and microfibril shape is better understood in Vaucheria. Each subunit of the diagonal row assembles a single glucan chain. Glucan chain products of the diagonal row aggregate to form an ordered aggregate. Aggregates unite laterally to form a thin ribbon-shaped microfibril. Whether or not the peculiar subunit geometry within the linear TC of Vaucheria is indicative of other xanthophycean algae is unknown at present. Vaucheria is yet but another example demonstrating the great diversity of cellulose biogenesis among the algae. With the rudimentary evidence at hand, one can now consider the evolution of cellulose biogenesis.

## THE EVOLUTION OF THE TC AND CELLULOSE BIOGENESIS

Based on TC ultrastructure and cellulose organisation, it is possible to construct a phylogenetic pathway for cellulose biogenesis. Although somewhat premature, this treatment gives several important and interesting clues to the subject of eukaryotic cellular evolution. Clearly, the algae as a group have been pivotal in the diversification of cellulose microfibril assembly as exemplified by the diversity of TC and microfibril morphology.

### Prokaryotic Cellulose

The evolution of cellulose among prokaryotic cells will first be considered. The fact that cellulose assembly occurs among two widely divergent prokaryotic groups suggests that this process must have been an ancient one. The investigations of Woese have shed much light on bacterial evolution. Using homologous sequences in rRNA, it has been possible to unambiguously examine and measure phylogenetic relationships among the bacteria

The genus, Sarcina is a gram + bacterium and is considered primitive among the eubacteria. Sarcina also is an obligate anaerobe. Cellulose synthesis in Sarcina was first described in 1961. We have also studied cellulose synthesis in Sarcina and have come to the conclusion that only the cellulose II polymorph is synthesized. The exact site of cellulose synthesis is unknown; however, membrane fractions of Sarcina can synthesize cellulose II in vitro.

Among the prokaryotes, the purple bacteria as a group are thought to be more advanced. They have been considered as progenitors of mitochondria in theeukaryotic cell. Interestingly, many genera in this group synthesize cellulose. These include, Acetobacter, Rhizobium, and Agrobacterium. As Woese points out, the purple bacteria are closely related and seem to have evolved special relationships with vascular plants as exemplified by nodules for nitrogen fixation in Rhizobium to tumors in Agrobacterium. The cellulose of Agrobacterium has been proposed to aid in establishing the virulence although it is not critical. The cellulose synthesized by Rhizobium may aid in attaching the bacterium to the root hair tip where it will initiate infection thread formation. In addition, cellulose is synthesized in Alcaligenes; however no cellulose synthesis has been observed in E. coli.

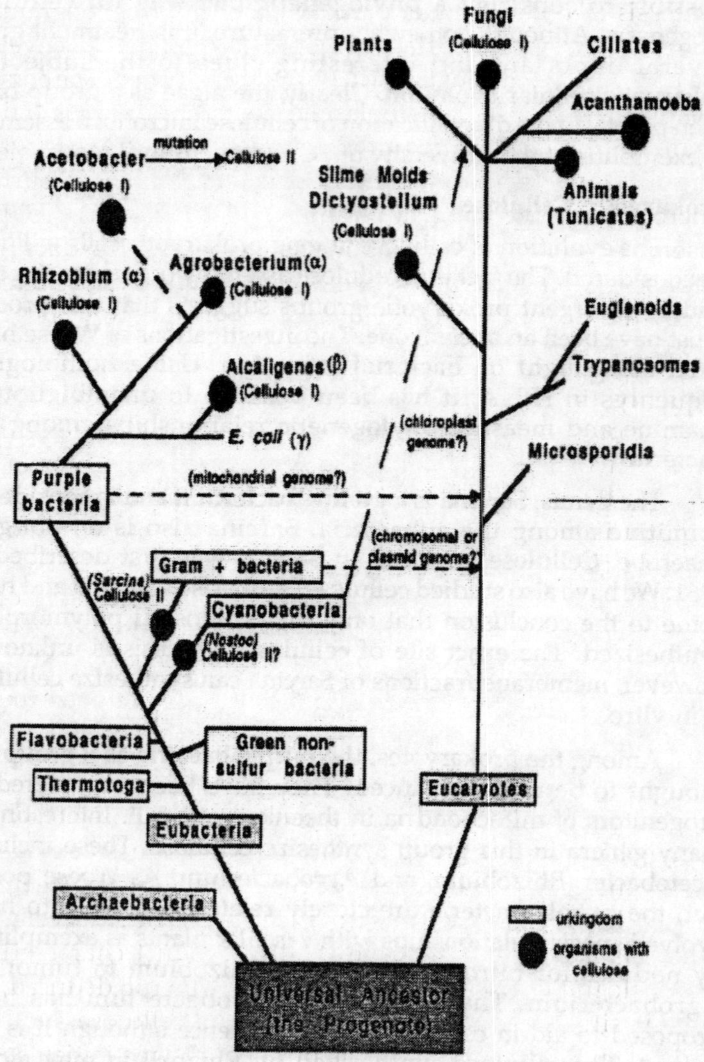


*Fig. 7.1:* Scheme of the evolution of cellulose synthesis based on the universal phylogenetic tree of woese.

Among the purple bacteria, only the cellulose I polymorph is synthesized (one exception is a mutation in Acetobacter giving rise to cellulose II synthesis. The site of cellulose microfibril synthesis is a linear row of particles parallel to the longitudinal axis of the cell. On the surface of the LPS layer of the cell envelope is a pore complex through which fibrils are extruded. The enzyme complex is located in the cytoplasmic membrane. Groups of three or more particles are required to assemble subfibrils which consolidate to form a microfibril tangential to the cell surface. Microfibrils unite to form bundles which, in turn, group to assemble ribbons. The ribbons are visible with darkfield microscopy, and the progress of cellulose synthesis can be directly monitored using time lapse video microscopy.

In Rhizobium and Agrobacterium, the sites of cellulose assembly are similar; however, fewer microfibrils consolidate. Only a floe of cellulose is produced, while in Acetobacter, a thick leathery membrane or pellicle is synthesized. The function of cellulose biosynthesis in - Acetobacter is unknown. Acetobacter xylinum is an obligate aerobe. Therefore the buoyancy of its cellulose could provide an aerobic environment for cells active in cellulose synthesis. Why Acetobacter ould divert large pools of metabolic substrate into cellulose is unknown; however, cellulose could serve as a reserve poolfor metabolism. Unfortunately, extensive cellulase activity has not been found; yet, degradation of non-crystalline carboxymethylcellulose can occur.

Fundamental research investigations of cellulose biogenesis in Acetobacter have yielded perhaps the most extensive evidence for the molecular mechanisms of cellulose assembly. Cellulose has now been synthesized in vitro; a specific activator for cellulose synthesis has been found, the in vitro product characterized morphologically, the in vitro crystalline polymorph deduced, the cellular site of the synthase localized, the cellulose synthase purified and gene cloning for the purified enzyme initiated.

Cellulose synthesis among the blue green algae has been mentioned only once in the literature, and conclusive evidence for this is lacking. The cyanobacteria emerged from the distance matrix phylogenetic tree of the eubacteria almost from the same region as the gram + bacteria and also close to the purple bacteria. Thus, it is clear that cellulose biogenesis must have been an ancient process during the evolution of life on earth.

With the accumulating evidence of cellulose biogenesis among prokaryotes, the evolution of cellulose among this group can now be addressed. The cellulose II polymorph appears to be primitive. This polymorph is the more thermodynamically stable form with an additional inter-chain H-bond formed per glucose residue. Cellulose II can form spontaneously from solution when cellulose is solubilized by such agents as DMSO/paraformaldehyde or cupraammonium reagents. On the other hand, cellulose I is a metastable polymorph, presumably assembled only by living organisms. Therefore, cellulose I is more advanced, requiring additional mechanisms for chain orientation and positioning to achieve the metastable state.

The first cellulose producer probably had its glucan synthase randomly organized in association with the memrane. Under these primitive conditions, only cellulose II could bioynthesized in vivo. Thus, in Sarcina, glucan chains appear to be randomly positioned over the cell surface in an amorphous array. Sarcina is an excellent example of an extant organism which lacks mechanisms to consolidate and organize the glucan synthase complex to induce ordered microfibril assembly and aggregation into bundles and ribbons of cellulose 1. On the other hand, the purple bacteria evolved the mechanisms to order glucan chains into various conformations leading to a diversity of cellulose I microfibril assembly. Because of abundant evidence suggesting that the purple bacteria are more advanced, it follows that cellulose I assembly is more advanced. A logical extension of this evolutionary advancement is to consider the evolution of cellulose among the eukaryotes. Did these cells obtain genes for cellulose synthesis from the eubacteria? If so, what are the likely candidates? It is obvious that if the mitochondria of eukaryotes came from the purple bacteria,did they also transfer the genes for organized cellulose I synthesis? This is an intriguing question, one which must await cloning and sequencing of the genes for the cellulose synthases.

## EUKARYOTIC CELLULOSE

We shall now consider one of the greatest mysteries in biology- the origin of cellulose synthesis among eukaryotic cells. The possibility that the genes for cellulose synthesis may have come from the purple bacteria has been alluded to. What was the first eukaryotic organism to have received the cellulose synthase gene? An examination of phylogenetic trees indicates that among the extant primitive eukaryotes, cellulose is found among one group, namely, the cellular slime molds. Cellulose I of low crystallinity has been found in Dictyostelium. Because Dictyostelium is non-photosynthetic, it seems highly unlikely that it could have received the genes for cellulose synthesis from a photosynthetic prokaryotic progenitor. It seems attractive, therefore, that the purple bacteria may have donated these complexes.

Dictyostelium TCs are unlike any so far found among eukaryotic cells. They appear to consist of linear arrays of single particl (Mizuta and Brown, unpublished results). These arrays are somewhat similar to those found in Acetobacter. Thus, among eukaryotic organisms, the linear arrangement of single rows of particle subunits (arrows) in Dictyostelium appears to be primitive. This is also supported by the low crystallinity of cellulose I from this organism.

Certain fungi, among them, the Oomycetes, synthesize cellulose. Yet, nothing is known of TC structure among the fungi. This is a major research area which needs immediate attention. One could predict, however, that if Vaucheria is closely related to Saprolegnia, the unique linear TC with diagonal rows might be found inthe latter.

Why many of the fungi opted for chitin as the major wall polymer is an interesting sidelight to the question of the evolution of cellulose synthesis. Some of the fungi are almost as primitive as Dictyostelium, yet there is scant knowledge of chitin synthesis among primitive eukaryotes, let alone the eubacteria and archaebacteria. Perhaps nutrition may have played a role in the more efficient utilization of strong polymers. Since chitin walled organisms may have required more nitrogen, the energy budget would be greater. Thus, to synthesize a polymer of cellulose would represent a selective advantage from a nutritional point of view.

## THE EVOLUTION OF CELLULOSE SYNTHESIS AMONG HOTO SYNTHETIC EUKARYOTES

At this junction, the algae certainly have played a diversified role, for it is here that the greatest variety of TCs and cellulose structure is found among the algae. Gunderson have suggested on the basis of18S rRNA sequences that a cellulose producing oomycete, Achlya bisexual is, is closely related to Ochromonas danica, a chitin producer. Perhaps the fungi and chromophytes appeared at roughly the same time.

On the basis of 28S cytoplasmic rRNA homology, they found that three distinct groups emerged late among eukaryotes: rhodophytes, chromophytes, and chlorophytes. A late occurrence of eukaryotic photosynthetic symbiosis was implied. The conserved rosette/linear TCs among the algae suggests that the synthase may have come from the more primitive fungior Dictyostelium, rather than through the chloroplast. Again, this implies that even earlier, the ancient eukaryotic mitochondrion may have contained the genes for cellulose synthase.

Could the cellulose synthase of the Rhodophyta have come from the cyanobacteria? This question cannot be answered until we have more data on the presence and physical characteristics of cellulose among the cyanobacteria. If only cellulose II is present among the cyanobacteria, it would be difficult to imagine an independent evolutionary event to organize the TC to allow it to produce cellulose I which is found among the Rhodophyta. If, however, Nostoc is foundto produce cellulose I in vivo, the hypothesis that the cyanobacteria could have been the progenitors of the Rhodophyta, would be strengthened. It should be apparent that these questions cannot really be answered, let alone seriously considered, until we have sequence information on the cellulose synthase; yet these questions do need to be placed before the scientific community now so that the blueprint for solving this great mystery can be expedited.

The origin of cellulose synthesis among the major algal groups is still a major mystery. Consider that cellulose is known among the Pyrrophyta, the Chrysophycease, the Xanthophyceae, the Phaeophyta, and the Chlorophyta Did each of these major groups receive a cellulose synthase independently, possibly from pro-chloroplast capture? The diversity of TC structure among these groups might suggest multiple independent captures, yet only the purple bacteria are known to synthesize cellulose I, the same polymorphfound among the great diversity of algae. This argues in favour of a single capture of the cellulose synthase very early in eukaryotic evolution, possibly through the purple bacteria donation of the pro-mitochondrial apparatus. This implies that the organisational machinery for glucan chain assembly into the cellulose I polymorph may have also been introduced early through transfer to an ancient eukaryotic progenitor. Then, Dictyostelium may be an example of one of the most ancient surviving groups which received the cellulose synthase from a prokaryotic progenitor. These are provocative questions, but ones which cannot be answered with certainty at present.

## CONCLUSIONS

Cellulose synthase is an ancient molecule as evidenced by its ubiquity among prokaryotic and eukaryotic organisms. It therefore must have served an important early function in the origin of life on earth. The most advanced eukaryotic land plants have the rosette cellulose synthase TC. Advanced members of the Charophyta have the rosette TC, an so do members of the Zygnemetales. At present, all pieces to the puzzle are not in place. Critically important algae need to be investigated for their TC structure to provide more direct confirming data for the rosette TC in land plant evolution. These include Coleochaetae, members of the Trentepholiales (Cephaleuros), the Klebsormidiales (Klebshormidium), the Chlorokybales (Chlorokybus), and other members of the Zygnematales ( Zygnema, Netrium).

The concept of symbiotic capture of the cellulose synthase in eukaryotic cells needs more study. Did the cellulose synthase come from a mitochondrial progenitor (through the purple bacteria)? Did it originate through a chloroplast progenitor (from

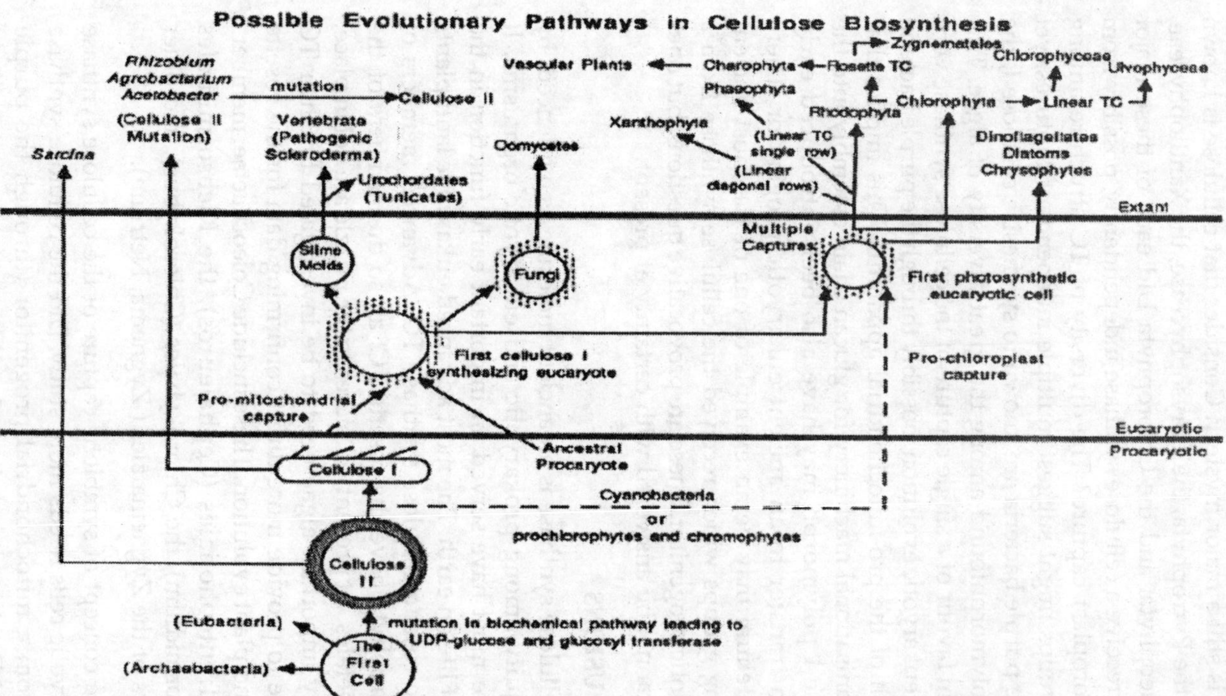


*Fig. 7.2:* **Possible evolutionary pathways of cellulose biogenesis, showing the rela**

the cyanobacteria, pro- chlorophyta, or pro-chromophyta)? Did the cellulose synthase transfer directly from the prokaryote chromosome or plasmid? Perhaps one or more symbiotic captures occurred, giving rise the the diversity of TC morphology and microfibril diversity.

The known diversity of cellulose microfibril structure, degree of polymerization, and crystallinity, suggests that secondary modifications to the primary glucan synthase must have occurred. Perhaps even the regulation of cellulose synthase activity has been modified, although cellulose synthase activity appears largely constitutive. The diversity of fibrillar polymers other than cellulose among the algae supports an extremely diverse evolution in cell wall structure, possibly reflecting the wide range of environments for survival.

Algae have served as excellent model systems in the quest for understanding cellulose biogenesis. Not only do the algae synthesize diverse forms off cellulose, they offer an uncompromising approach for cytological observation, coupled with a potential for isolation, cloning, and sequencing of the genes involved in cellulose biogenesis. The coming decade will see great advances in cellulose biogenesis research.

# Chapter–8

# Oomycete

## INTRODUCTION

Oomycetes also known as Water molds (or *water moulds*: see spelling differences) are a group of filamentous, unicellular Heterokonts, physically resembling fungi. They are microscopic, absorptive organisms that reproduce both sexually and asexually and are composed of mycelia, or a tube-like vegetative body (all of an organism's mycelia are called its thallus). The name "water mold" refers to their earlier classification as fungi, which stemmed from their preference for conditions of high humidity and running surface water, although they are now known to have evolved separately and show a number of differences. For instance, their cell walls are composed of cellulose rather than chitin and generally do not have septations. Also, in the vegetative state they have diploid nuclei, whereas fungi have haploid nuclei.

Instead, water molds are related to organisms such as brown algae and diatoms, making up a group called the heterokonts. The name comes from the common arrangement and structure of motile cells, which typically have two unequal flagella. Among the water molds, these are produced as asexual spores called zoospores, which capitalize on surface water (including precipitation on plant surfaces) for movement. They also produce sexual spores, called oospores, that are translucent double-walled spherical structures used to survive adverse environmental conditions. A few produce aerial asexual spores that are distributed by wind.

The water molds are economically and scientifically important because they are aggressive plant pathogens . Some species can cause disease in fish. The majority can be broken down into three groups, although more exist.

- The *Phytophthora* group is a genus that causes diseases such as dieback, late blight in potatoes (the cause of the Great Hunger or Potato Famine of the 1840s in Ireland), sudden oak death, rhododendron root rot, and Ink Disease in the American Chestnut.
- The *Pythium* group is even more prevalent than *Phytophythora* and individual species have larger host ranges, usually causing less damage. *Pythium* damping off is a very common problem in greenhouses where the organism kills newly emerged seedlings. Mycoparasitic members of this group (e.g. *P. oligandrum*) parasitize other oomycetes and fungi, and have been employed as biocontrol agents. One *Pythium* species, *Pythium insidiosum* is also known to infect mammals. water mold comes from everywhere and you can find it in jungles and other places.
- The third group are the downy mildews, which are easily identifiable by the appearance of white "mildew" on leaf surfaces (although this group can be confused with the unrelated powdery mildews).

## CLASSIFICATION OF OOMYCETES

Traditionally, this group was thought to include types of fungi, and indeed fungi themselves were once believed to be closely related to plants. However, further research has concluded that this is not true and that fungi are more closely related to animals. Many species of Oomycetes are still described or listed as types of fungi and may sometimes be referred to as pseudofungi, or lower fungi. Oomycetes are actually members of the chromistans, which are in turn part of the larger Kingdom Protoctista.

### Phytophthora

*Phytophthora* (from Greek phytón, "plant" and phthorá, "destruction"; "the plant-destroyer") is a genus of plant-damaging Protists of the *Oomycetes* (water molds). Heinrich Anton de Bary described it for the first time in 1875.

**Pathogens**

*Phytophthoras* are mostly pathogens of dicotyledons, and are relatively host-specific parasites. Many species of *Phytophthora* are plant pathogens of considerable economic importance. *Phytophthora infestans* was the infective agent of the potato blight that caused the Great Irish Famine (1845-1849). Plant diseases caused by this genus are difficult to control chemically, thus resistant cultivars are grown as a management strategy. Research beginning in the 1990s has placed some of the responsibility for European forest die-back on the activity of imported Asian *Phytophthoras*.

Other important *Phytophthora* diseases are:

- *Phytophthora alni* – causes alder root rot.
- *Phytophthora cactorum* – causes rhododendron root rot affecting rhododendrons, azaleas and causes bleeding canker in hardwood trees.
- *Phytophthora cinnamomi* - causes cinnamon root rot affecting woody ornamentals including arborvitae, azalea, Chamaecyparis, dogwood, forsythia, Fraser fir, hemlock, Japanese holly, juniper, Pieris, rhododendron, Taxus, white pine, and American chestnut.
- *Phytophthora fragariae* - causes red root rot affecting strawberries.
- *Phytophthora palmivora* - causes fruit rot in coconuts and betel nuts.
- *Phytophthora ramorum* – infects over 60 plant genera and over 100 host species - causes Sudden Oak Death.
- *Phytophthora quercina* – causes oak death.
- *Phytophthora sojae* - causes soybean root rot.

**FUNGI RESEMBLANCE**

*Phytophthora* is sometimes referred to as a fungal-like organism but it is classified under a different kingdom altogether:

Stramenopila (previously named Chromista). This is a good example of convergent evolution: *Phytophthora* is morphologically very similar to true fungi yet its evolutionary history is quite distinct. In contrast to fungi, stramenopiles are more closely related to plants than animals. Whereas fungal cell walls are made primarily of chitin, stramenopile cell walls are constructed mostly of cellulose. Ploidy levels are different between these two kingdoms as are biochemical pathways.

**Biology**

*Phytophthoras* may reproduce sexually or asexually. In many species, sexual structures have never been observed, or have only been observed in laboratory matings. In homothallic species, sexual structures occur in single culture. Heterothallic species have mating strains, designated as A1 and A2. When mated, antheridia introduce gametes into oogonia, either by the oogonium passing through the antheridium (amphigyny) or by the antheridium attaching to the proximal (lower) half of the oogonium (paragyny), and the union producing oospores. Like animals, but not like most true Fungi, meiosis is gametic, and somatic nuclei are diploid. Asexual (mitotic) spore types are chlamydospores, and sporangia which produce zoospores. Chlamydospores are usually spherical and pigmented, and may have a thickened cell wall to aid in its role as a survival structure. Sporangia may be retained by the subtending hyphae (non-caducous) or be shed readily by wind or water tension (caducous) acting as dispersal structures. Also, sporangia may release zoospores, which have two unlike flagella which they use to swim towards a host plant.

***Species***

*Phytophthora* arecae

*Phytophthora* botryosa

*Phytophthora* brassicae

*Phytophthora* cactorum

*Phytophthora* cajani

| | |
|---|---|
| *Phytophthora* | cambivora |
| *Phytophthora* | capsici |
| *Phytophthora* | cinnamomi |
| *Phytophthora* | citricola |
| *Phytophthora* | citrophthora |
| *Phytophthora* | clandestina |
| *Phytophthora* | colocasiae |
| *Phytophthora* | cryptogea |
| *Phytophthora* | drechsleri |
| *Phytophthora* | erythroseptica |
| *Phytophthora* | fragariae |
| *Phytophthora* | gonapodyides |
| *Phytophthora* | heveae |
| *Phytophthora* | humicola |
| *Phytophthora* | idaei |
| *Phytophthora* | ilicis |
| *Phytophthora* | infestans |
| *Phytophthora* | inflata |
| *Phytophthora* | iranica |
| *Phytophthora* | katsurae |
| *Phytophthora* | lateralis |
| *Phytophthora* | medicaginis |
| *Phytophthora* | megakarya |
| *Phytophthora* | megasperma |
| *Phytophthora* | melonis |
| *Phytophthora* | mirabilis |
| *Phytophthora* | multivesiculata |

| | |
|---|---|
| *Phytophthora* | nicotianae |
| *Phytophthora* | palmivora |
| *Phytophthora* | phaseoli |
| *Phytophthora* | porri |
| *Phytophthora* | primulae |
| *Phytophthora* | pseudotsugae |
| *Phytophthora* | quercina |
| *Phytophthora* | ramorum |
| *Phytophthora* | sinensis |
| *Phytophthora* | sojae |
| *Phytophthora* | syringae |
| *Phytophthora* | tentaculata |
| *Phytophthora* | trifolii |
| *Phytophthora* | vignae |

## PYTHIUM

Pythium is a genus of parasitic oomycete. Because this group of organisms were once classified as fungi, they are sometimes still treated as such.

*Pythium*, like others in the family *Pythiaceae*, are usually characterized by their production of coenocytic hyphae, hyphae without septations.

- Oogonia

  Generally contain a single oospore
- Antheridia

  Contain an elongated and club-shaped antheridium.

### Ecological Importance

*Pythium* root rot is a common crop disease caused by a genus of organisms called "Pythium". These are commonly called water moulds. *Pythium* damping off is a very common problem in fields and greenhouses, where the organism kills newly emerged seedlings. This disease complex usually involves other pathogens such as *Phytophthora* and *Rhizoctonia*. Pythium wilt is caused by zoospore infection of older plants leading to biotrophic infections that become necrotrophic in response to colonization/reinfection pressures or environmental stress, leading to minor or severe wilting caused by impeded root functioning.

Many *Pythium* species, along with their close relatives, *Phytophthora* species are plant pathogens of economic importance in agriculture. *Pythium* spp. tend to be very generalistic and unspecific in their host range. They infect a large range of hosts, while *Phytophthora* spp. are generally more host-specific.

For this reason, *Pythium* spp. are more devastating in the root rot they cause in crops, because crop rotation alone will often not eradicate the pathogen (nor will fallowing the field, as *Pythium* spp. are also good saprotrophs, and will survive for a long time on decaying plant matter).

It has been noted that in field crops, damage by *Pythium* spp. is often limited to the area affected, as the motile zoospores require ample surface water to travel long distances. Additionally, the capillaries formed by soil particles act as a natural filter and effectively trap many zoospores. However, in hydroponic systems inside greenhouses, where extensive monocultures of plants are maintained in plant nutrient solution (containing nitrogen, potassium, phosphate, and micronutrients) that is continuously recirculated to the crop, *Pythium* spp. cause extensive and devastating root rot and is often difficult to prevent or control. The root rot affects entire operations (tens of thousands of plants, in many instances) within two to four days due to the inherent nature of hydroponic systems where roots are nakedly exposed to the water medium, in which the zoospores can move freely.

Several *Pythium* species, including *P. oligandrum*, *P. nunn*, *P. periplocum*, and *P. acanthicum* are mycoparasites of plant pathogenic fungi and oomycetes, and have received interest as potential biocontrol agents.

***Species***

| | |
|---|---|
| *Pythium* | acanthicum |
| *Pythium* | acanthophoron |
| *Pythium* | acrogynum |
| *Pythium* | adhaerens |
| *Pythium* | amasculinum |
| *Pythium* | anandrum |
| *Pythium* | angustatum |
| *Pythium* | aphanidermatum |
| *Pythium* | apleroticum |
| *Pythium* | aquatile |
| *Pythium* | aristosporum |
| *Pythium* | arrhenomanes |
| *Pythium* | attrantheridium |
| *Pythium* | bifurcatum |
| *Pythium* | boreale |
| *Pythium* | buismaniae |
| *Pythium* | butleri |
| *Pythium* | campanulatum |
| *Pythium* | canariense |
| *Pythium* | capillosum |
| *Pythium* | carbonicum |
| *Pythium* | carolinianum |
| *Pythium* | catenulatum |
| *Pythium* | chamaehyphon |
| *Pythium* | chondricola |
| *Pythium* | citrinum |

| | |
|---|---|
| *Pythium* | coloratum |
| *Pythium* | conidiophorum |
| *Pythium* | contiguanum |
| *Pythium* | cryptoirregulare |
| *Pythium* | cucurbitacearum |
| *Pythium* | cylindrosporum |
| *Pythium* | cystogenes |
| *Pythium* | debaryanum |
| *Pythium* | deliense |
| *Pythium* | destruens |
| *Pythium* | diclinum |
| *Pythium* | dimorphum |
| *Pythium* | dissimile |
| *Pythium* | dissotocum |
| *Pythium* | echinulatum |
| *Pythium* | erinaceum |
| *Pythium* | flevoense |
| *Pythium* | folliculosum |
| *Pythium* | glomeratum |
| *Pythium* | graminicola |
| *Pythium* | grandisporangium |
| *Pythium* | guiyangense |
| *Pythium* | helicandrum |
| *Pythium* | helicoides |
| *Pythium* | heterothallicum |
| *Pythium* | hydnosporum |
| *Pythium* | hypogynum |
| *Pythium* | indigoferae |

| | |
|---|---|
| *Pythium* | inflatum |
| *Pythium* | insidiosum |
| *Pythium* | intermedium |
| *Pythium* | irregulare |
| *Pythium* | iwayamai |
| *Pythium* | jasmonium |
| *Pythium* | kunmingense |
| *Pythium* | litorale |
| *Pythium* | longandrum |
| *Pythium* | longisporangium |
| *Pythium* | lutarium |
| *Pythium* | macrosporum |
| *Pythium* | mamillatum |
| *Pythium* | marinum |
| *Pythium* | marsipium |
| *Pythium* | mastophorum |
| *Pythium* | megacarpum |
| *Pythium* | megalacanthum |
| *Pythium* | middletonii |
| *Pythium* | minus |
| *Pythium* | monospermum |
| *Pythium* | montanum |
| *Pythium* | multisporum |
| *Pythium* | myriotylum |
| *Pythium* | nagaii |
| *Pythium* | nodosum |
| *Pythium* | nunn |
| *Pythium* | oedochilum |

| | |
|---|---|
| *Pythium* | okanoganense |
| *Pythium* | oligandrum |
| *Pythium* | ornacarpum |
| *Pythium* | orthogonon |
| *Pythium* | ostracodes |
| *Pythium* | pachycaule |
| *Pythium* | pachycaule |
| *Pythium* | paddicum |
| *Pythium* | paroecandrum |
| *Pythium* | parvum |
| *Pythium* | pectinolyticum |
| *Pythium* | periilum |
| *Pythium* | periplocum |
| *Pythium* | perplexum |
| *Pythium* | phragmitis |
| *Pythium* | pleroticum |
| *Pythium* | plurisporium |
| *Pythium* | polymastum |
| *Pythium* | porphyrae |
| *Pythium* | prolatum |
| *Pythium* | proliferatum |
| *Pythium* | pulchrum |
| *Pythium* | pyrilobum |
| *Pythium* | quercum |
| *Pythium* | radiosum |
| *Pythium* | ramificatum |
| *Pythium* | regulare |

| | |
|---|---|
| *Pythium* | rhizo-oryzae |
| *Pythium* | rhizosaccharum |
| *Pythium* | rostratifingens |
| *Pythium* | rostratum |
| *Pythium* | salpingophorum |
| *Pythium* | scleroteichum |
| *Pythium* | segnitium |
| *Pythium* | spiculum |
| *Pythium* | spinosum |
| *Pythium* | splendens |
| *Pythium* | sterilum |
| *Pythium* | sulcatum |
| *Pythium* | sylvaticum |
| *Pythium* | terrestris |
| *Pythium* | torulosum |
| *Pythium* | tracheiphilum |
| *Pythium* | ultimum |
| *Pythium* | uncinulatum |
| *Pythium* | undulatum |
| *Pythium* | vanterpoolii |
| *Pythium* | vexans |
| *Pythium* | viniferum |
| *Pythium* | violae |
| *Pythium* | volutum |
| *Pythium* | zingiberis |
| *Pythium* | zingiberum |

## POWDERY MILDEW

Powdery mildew is a fungal disease that affects a wide range of plants. Powdery mildew diseases are caused by many different species of fungi in the order Erysiphales. It is one of the easier diseases to spot, as its symptoms are quite distinctive. Infected plants display white powder-like spots on the leaves and stems. The lower leaves are the most affected, but the mildew can appear on any part of the plant that shows above the ground. As the disease progresses, the spots get larger and thicker as massive numbers of spores form, and the mildew spreads up and down the length of the plant.

### Powdery Mildews of Various Plants

#### *Powdery Mildew of Grape*

*Erysiphe necator* (or *Uncinula necator*) causes powdery mildew of grapes. It produces common odors such as 1-octen-3-one and (Z)-1,5-octadien-3-one.

#### *Powdery Mildew of Wheat and Barley*

*Blumeria graminis*, the fungus that causes powdery mildew of grasses, can persist between seasons in wheat stubble that is left in the field, or in wheat that is left to overwinter. It thrives in cool humid conditions. Controlling the disease involves eliminating those conditions as much as possible. Wheat plants should not be overcrowded in the field. This allows better air circulation among the lower parts of the plants, which lowers the humidity levels. Nitrogen fertilizers encourage lots of leafy growth, and in farming systems that use them they should be used sparingly to control powdery mildew. Crop rotation with non-host plants is another way to keep mildew infection to a minimum. Reducing splash from contaminated soil also helps control spores. Chemical control is possible with anti-fungals such as triademefon and propiconazole. Some farmers are experimenting with spraying plants with waste milk, with varying degrees of success.

#### *Powdery Mildew of Onions*

The fungus causing powdery mildew of onions is *Leveillula taurica* (also known by its anamorph name, *Oidiopsis taurica*). It also attacks the artichoke.

### *Cure for Powdery Mildew*

Left untreated, powdery mildew will kill your plant. Common fungicides bought at a local garden store will help by either killing the fungus or by not allowing the fungus to make spores and reproduce. When applying, be sure to spray the leaf, the underside of the leaf, the stem connecting the leaf to the vine, and the vine itself. These fungicides, though, are not cheap and there are some natural ways to treat the powdery mildew. Baking Soda is a very versatile, readily available, and relatively inexpensive; it also can help control and even cure Powdery Mildew. A mixture of one tablespoon Baking Soda, 2.5 tablespoons vegetable oil, and 4-5 drops of liquid soap added to a gallon of water will act as a fine, natural, and inexpensive fungicide (be sure to agitate spray bottle regularly while applying to keep the ingredients from separating). Another natural cure for this mildew is a mixture of one part milk (any kind or brand) to three parts water.

### *Reproduction of Powdery Mildew*

Powdery Mildew reproduces through what is known as cleistothesium. This structure is circular in shape and is a totally enclosed ascocarp. This is a dense, hard, fungal mass created from fungal tissues. The ascocarp cracks open and releases bodies called asci (singular Ascus). These asci hold the ascospores the 'seed' of the fungus.

## HETEROKONT

The heterokonts or stramenopiles are a major line of eukaryotes presently containing about 10,500 known species.[1] Most are algae, ranging from the giant multicellular kelp to the unicellular diatoms, which are a primary component of plankton. Other notable members of the Stramenopila include the (generally parasitic) oomycetes, including *Phytophthora* of Irish potato famine infamy and *Pythium* which causes seed rot and damping off.

### Chloroplasts

Heterokont algae are chromists with chloroplasts surrounded by four membranes, which are counted from the outermost to the innermost membrane. The first membrane is continuous with the host's chloroplast endoplasmic reticulum, or cER. The second membrane presents a barrier between the lumen of the endoplasmic reticulum and the primary endosymbiont or chloroplast, which represents the next two membranes, within which the thylakoid membranes are found. This arrangement of membranes suggest that heterokont chloroplasts were obtained from the reduction of a symbiotic red algal eukaryote, which had arisen by evolutionary divergence from the monophyletic primary endosymbiotic ancestor that is thought to have given rise to all eukaryotic photoautotrophs. The chloroplasts characteristically contain chlorophyll a and chlorophyll c, and usually the accessory pigment fucoxanthin, giving them a golden-brown or brownish-green colour.

Most basal heterokonts are colourless, suggesting they diverged before aqcuisition of chloroplasts within the group. However, fucoxanthin-containing chloroplasts are also found among the haptophytes, and evidence suggests that the two groups have a common ancestry, as well as possible a common phylogenetic history with cryptomonads. In this case the ancestral heterokont was an alga, and all colourless groups arose through loss of the secondary endosymbiont and hence its chloroplast.

**Motile Cells**

Many heterokonts are unicellular flagellates, and most others produce flagellate cells at some point in their life-cycle, for instance as gametes or zoospores. The name heterokont refers to the characteristic form of these cells, which typically have two unequal flagella. The anterior or *tinsel* flagellum is covered with lateral bristles or *mastigonemes*, while the other flagellum is whiplash, smooth and usually shorter, or sometimes reduced to a basal body. The flagella are inserted subapically or laterally, and are usually supported by four microtubule roots in a distinctive pattern.

Mastigonemes are manufactured from glycoproteins in the cell's endoplasmic reticulum before being transported to its surface. When the tinsel flagellum moves, these create a backwards current, pulling the cell through the water or bringing in food. The mastigonemes have a peculiar tripartite structure, which may be taken as the defining characteristic of the group, thereby including a few protists that do not produce cells with the typical heterokont form. They have been lost in a few lines, most notably the diatoms.

**Classification**

As noted above, classification varies considerably. Originally the heterokont algae were treated as two divisions, first within the kingdom Plantae and later the Protista:

In this scheme, however, the Chrysophyceae are paraphyletic to both other groups. As a result, various members have been given their own classes and often divisions. Recent systems often treat these as classes within a single division, called the Heterokontophyta, Chromophyta or Ochrophyta. This is not universal, however - for instance Round *et al.* treat the diatoms as a division.

The discovery that oomycetes and hyphochytrids are related to these algae, rather than fungi as previously thought, has led many authors to include them among the heterokonts. Should it turn out that they evolved from coloured ancestors, the group would be paraphyletic in their absence. Once again, however, usage varies. David J. Patterson named this extended group the stramenopiles, characterized by the presence of tripartite mastigonemes, mitochondria with tubular cristae, and open mitosis. He used the stramenopiles as a prototype for a classification without Linnaean ranks. Their composition has been essentially stable, but their use within ranked systems varies.

Thomas Cavalier-Smith treats the heterokonts as identical in composition with the stramenopiles; this is the definition followed here. He has proposed placing them in a separate kingdom Chromalveolata, together with the haptophytes, cryptomonads and alveolates. This is one of the most common revisions to the five-kingdom system, but has not been generally adopted, partly because some biologists doubt their monophyly. A few treat the Chromalveolata as identical in composition with the heterokonts, or list them as a kingdom Stramenopila.

**Rationale for "stramenopile"**

The origin of the name stramenopile is explained by Adl and coauthors:

> Regarding the spelling of stramenopile, it was originally spelled stramenopile. The Latin word for "straw" is stramine-us, -a, -um, adj. [stramen], made of straw—thus, it should have been spelled straminopile. However, Patterson (1989) clearly stated that this is a common name (hence, lower case, not capitalized) and as a common name, it can be spelled as Patterson chooses. If he had stipulated that the name was a formal name, governed by rules of nomenclature, then his spelling would have been an orthogonal mutation and one would simply correct the spelling in subsequent publications (e.g. Straminopiles). But, it was not Patterson's desire to use the term in a formal sense. Thus, if we use it in a formal sense, it must be formally described (and in addition, in Latin, if it is to be used botanically). However, and here is the strange part of this, many people liked the name, but wanted it to be used formally. So they capitalized the ?rst letter, and made it Stramenopiles; others corrected the Latin spelling to Straminopiles.

# Chapter–9

# Slime Mold

## INTRODUCTION

Slime Mold is a broad term that refers to fungi-like amoeboid (i.e. like an amoeba) organisms. Their common name refers to part of their life cycle in which their appearance can be gelatinous (hence the name slime). However, this fact mostly refers to the myxomycetes, which are the only macroscopic slime molds. They have been found all over the world feeding on microorganisms that live in any type of dead plant material. For this reason, it is very common to find these organisms growing in the soil, on lawns, and in the forest commonly on deciduous logs (hence the name molds). However, in tropical areas of the world, they also seem to be very common on inflorescences, fruits and in aerial situations (i.e. in the canopy of trees). They are also common on mulch or even in the leaf mold in gutters.

## TAXONOMY

Slime molds as a group (*sensu lato*) are polyphyletic. They were originally represented by the subkingdom Gymnomycota in the Fungi kingdom and included the defunct phyla Myxomycota, Acrasiomycota and Labyrinthulomycota. Today, slime molds have been divided between four supergroups and paradoxically none of them is included in the Fungi. These are:

- Mycetozoa, which includes the defunct phylum Myxomycota, belong to the supergroup Amoebozoa and include:

- Myxogastria or myxomycetes and Protosteli syncytial or plasmodial slime molds or protostelids.
- *Dictyosteliida:* unicellular slime molds or dictyostelids.
- *Acrasiomycota:* slime molds which belong to the supergroup Excavata as the family Acrasidae. They have a similar life style to Dictyostelids.
- *Labyrinthulomycota:* slime nets which belong to the supergroup Chromalveolata as the class Labyrinthulomycetes.
- *Plasmodiophorids:* parasitic protists which belong to the supergroup Rhizaria. They can cause cabbage club root disease and powdery scab tuber disease.

In more strict terms (*sensu stricto*) slime molds conform the group of the mycetozoans (myxomycetes, dictyostelids and protostelids). However, even at this level there are conflicts yet to be resolved. Recent molecular evidence shows that the first two groups are likely to be monophytelic, however the protostelids seem to be polyphyletic too. For this reason, scientists are trying to elucidate the relations between these three groups.

## LIFE CYCLE

They begin life as amoeba-like cells. These unicellular amoebae are commonly haploid and multiply if they encounter their favorite food, bacteria. These amoebae can mate if they encounter the correct mating type and form zygotes which then grow into plasmodia which contain many nuclei without cell membranes between them, which can grow to be meters in size. One variety is often seen as a slimy yellow network in and on rotting logs. The amoebae and the plasmodia engulf microorganisms. The plasmodium grows into an interconnected network of protoplasmic strands.

Within each protoplasmic strand the cytoplasmic contents rapidly stream. If one strand is carefully watched for about 50 seconds the cytoplasm can be seen to slow, stop, and then reverse direction. The streaming protoplasm within a plasmodial strand can reach speeds of up to 1.35 mm per second which is the fastest rate recorded for any organism. Migration of the plasmodium is accomplished when more protoplasm streams to advancing areas and protoplasm is withdrawn from rear areas. When the food supply wanes, the plasmodium will migrate to the surface of its substrate and transform into rigid fruiting bodies. The fruiting bodies or sporangia are what we commonly see, superficially look like fungi or molds but they are not related to the true fungi. These sporangia will then release spores which hatch into amoebae to begin the life cycle again.

## TYPES OF SLIME MOLD

Most slime mold are smaller than a few centimetres, but the very largest reach areas of up to thirty square metres, making them the largest undivided cells known. Many have striking colours such as yellow, brown and white.

Slime molds can generally be divided into two main groups. A plasmodial slime mold involves numerous individual cells attached to each other, forming one large membrane. This "supercell" is essentially a bag of cytoplasm containing thousands of individual nuclei. By contrast, cellular slime molds spend most of their lives as individual unicellular protists, but when a chemical signal is secreted, they assemble into a cluster that acts as one organism.

A common slime mold which forms tiny brown tufts on rotting logs is *Stemonitis*. Another form which lives in rotting logs and is often used in research is *Physarum polycephalum*. In logs it has the appearance of a slimy webwork of yellow threads, up to a few feet in size. *Fuligo* forms yellow crusts in mulch.

The Protostelids' life cycle is very similar to the above descriptions, but they are much smaller, the fruiting bodies only forming one to a few spores.

The Dictyosteliida, cellular slime molds, are distantly related to the plasmodial slime molds and have a very different life style. Their amoebae do not form huge coenocytes, and remain individual. They live in similar habitats and feed on microorganisms. When food runs out and they are ready to form sporangia, they do something radically different. They release signal molecules into their environment, by which they find each other and create swarms. These amoeba then join up into a tiny multicellular slug-like coordinated creature, which crawls to an open lit place and grows into a fruiting body. Some of the amoebae become spores to begin the next generation, but some of the amoebae sacrifice themselves to become a dead stalk, lifting the spores up into the air.

The Acrasidae have a life style similar to Dictyostelids, but their amoebae behave differently and are of uncertain taxonomic position.

The Plasmodiophorids also form coenocytes but are internal parasites of plants (e.g., club root disease of cabbages).

Finally, the Labyrinthulomycetes are marine and form labyrinthine networks of tubes in which amoebae without pseudopods can travel.

**SLIME MOLDS IN CULTURE**

Although usually overlooked, slime molds have occasionally found their way into art and literature. Traditional Finnish lore describes how malicious witches used yellow Fuligo (there called "paranvoi," or butter of the familiar) to spoil milk. In many popular roguelikes, as a hold-over from the original *Rogue,* "slime mold" is the default name of a food item. Whether or not most actual slime molds are delicious, or even edible, is unclear, and some may be poisonous. However, mycologist Tom Volk reports that the plasmodium of *Fuligo* is eaten in Mexico. The graphic novel *Nausicaä of the Valley of Wind* features a highly dangerous mutated slime mold that engulfs entire cities. Philip K. Dick's novel Clans of the Alphane Moon contains a character called Lord Running Clam, a "Ganymedean Slime Mold" who talks and is very intelligent and has telepathic powers. In Jeffrey Darlington's comic General Protection Fault, one character's poor hygiene leads to the development of a sentient species of slime mold in his apartment that split the rent with him. In the DVD release of *This is Spinal Tap* there is an outtake of an interview with David St. Hubbins in which he speaks of slime molds: "Slime molds are so close to being both plant and animal... that it's like they can't make up their minds . . . and they're thinking now that maybe it's this, is who's been running the earth all this time."

# Chapter–10

# Kinetoplastid

## INTRODUCTION

The kinetoplastids are a group of flagellate protozoa, including a number of parasites responsible for serious diseases in humans and other animals, as well as various forms found in soil and aquatic environments. They are included in the Euglenozoa, and are distinguished from other such forms mainly by the presence of a *kinetoplast*, a DNA-containing granule located within the single mitochondrion and associated with the flagellar bases.

Most forms have a leading and trailing flagellum, the latter of which may or may not be attached to the side of the cell and is often used to glide along or attach to surfaces. The cytostome is often bordered by a ridge or rostrum. *Bodo* is a typical genus, including various common free-living species which feed on bacteria. Others include *Cryptobia* and *Trypanoplasma*. There is also one family of kinetoplastids, the trypanosomes, which only have a single emergent flagellum, including several genera which are exclusively parasitic.

Trypanosomes have reduced or absent cytostomes, feeding entirely through absorption, and smaller kinetoplasts than other forms. They typically have complex life-cycles involving more than one host, and go through various morphological stages. The most distinctive of these are the Trypomastigote stages, where the flagellum runs along the length of the cell and is connected to it forming an undulating membrane. Diseases caused by trypanosomes include sleeping sickness and Chagas disease, from species of *Trypanosoma*, and leishmaniasis, from species of *Leishmania*.

The kinetoplastids were first defined by Honigberg in 1961 as the flagellate order Kinetoplastid . They are traditionally divided into the biflagellate Bodonidae and uniflagellate Trypanosomatidae, which may be promoted to orders; the former appears to be paraphyletic to the latter.

## PARASITISM

Parasitism is a type of symbiotic relationship between two different organisms. The parasite benefits from a prolonged, close association with the host, which is harmed. In general, parasites are much smaller than their hosts, show a high degree of specialization for their mode of life and reproduce more quickly and in greater numbers than their hosts. Classic examples of parasitism include the interactions between vertebrate hosts and such diverse animals as the tapeworms, flukes, *Plasmodium* species and scabs.

The harm and benefit in parasitic interactions concern the biological fitness of the organisms involved. Parasites reduce host fitness in many ways, ranging from general or specialized pathology (such as castration), impairment of secondary sex characteristics, to the modification of host behaviour. Parasites increase their fitness by exploiting hosts for food, habitat and dispersal.

Although the concept of parasitism applies unambiguously to many cases in nature, it is best considered part of a continuum of types of interactions between species, rather than an exclusive category. Particular interactions between species may satisfy some but not all parts of the definition. In many cases, it is difficult to demonstrate that the host is harmed. In others, there may be no apparent specialization on the part of the parasite, or the interaction between the organisms may be short-lived. In medicine, only eukaryotic organisms are considered parasites, to the exclusion of bacteria and viruses. Some branches of biology, however, do regard members of these groups to be parasitic.

**Types of Parasitism**

Parasites are classified based on a variety of aspects of their interactions with their hosts and on their life cycles. Those that live inside the host are called endoparasites (e.g., hookworms) and those that live on its surface are called ectoparasites (e.g., some mites). An epiparasite is one that feeds on another parasite. This relationship is also sometimes referred to as "hyperparasitism". A female *Catolaccus grandis* wasp homes in on a boll weevil larva.

Parasitoids are organisms whose larval development occurs within another organism's body, resulting in the death of the host. Thus, the interaction between the parasitoid and the host is fundamentally different than true parasites and their host, and shares some characteristics with predation. Social parasites take advantage of interactions between members of social organisms such as ants or termites. In kleptoparasitism, parasites appropriate food gathered by the host. An example is the brood parasitism practiced by many species of cuckoo. Many cuckoos use other bird species as "babysitters", depositing their eggs in the nest of the host species, which raise the cuckoo young as one of their own.

Parasitism can take the form of isolated cheating or exploitation among more generalized mutualistic interactions. For example, broad classes of plants and fungi exchange carbon and nutrients in common mutualistic mycorrhizal relationships; however, a few plants species (known as myco-heterotrophs) "cheat" by taking carbon from a fungus rather than donating it.

Biotrophic parasitism is an extremely common mode of life that has arisen independently many times in the course of evolution. Depending on the definition used, as many as half of all animals have at least one parasitic phase in their life cycles and it is also frequent in plants and fungi. Moreover, almost all free-living animals are host to one or more parasite taxa.

Parasites evolve in response to defense mechanisms of their hosts. Examples of host defenses include the toxins produced by plants to deter parasitic fungi and bacteria, the complex vertebrate immune system, which can target parasites through contact with bodily fluids, and behavioural defenses. An example of the latter is the avoidance by sheep of open pastures during spring, when roundworm eggs accumulated over the previous year hatch en masse. As a result of these and other host defenses, some parasites evolve adaptations that are specific to a particular host taxon and specialize to the point where they infect only a single species. Such narrow host specificity can be costly over evolutionary time, however, if the host species becomes extinct. Thus, many parasites are capable of infecting a variety of host species that are more or less closely related, with varying success.

Host defenses also evolve in response to attacks by parasites. Theoretically, parasites may have an advantage in this evolutionary arms race because of their more rapid generation time. Hosts reproduce less quickly than parasites, and therefore have fewer chances to adapt than their parasites do over a given span of time.

In some cases, a parasite species may coevolve with its host taxa. In theory, long-term coevolution should lead to a relatively stable relationship tending to commensalism or mutualism, in that it is in the evolutionary interest of the parasite that its host thrives. A parasite may evolve to become less harmful for its host or a host may evolve to cope with the unavoidable presence of a parasite to the point that the parasite's absence causes the host harm. For example, although animals infected with parasitic worms are often clearly harmed, and therefore parasitized, such infections may also reduce the prevalence and effects of autoimmune disorders in animal hosts, including humans.

The presumption of a shared evolutionary history between parasites and hosts can sometimes elucidate how host taxa are related. For instance, there has been dispute about whether flamingos are more closely related to the storks and their allies or to ducks, geese and their relatives. The fact that flamingos share parasites with ducks and geese is evidence these groups may be more closely related to each other than either is to storks.

Parasitism is part of one explanation for the evolution of secondary sex characteristics seen in breeding males throughout the animal world, such as the plumage of male peacocks and manes of male lions. According to this theory, female hosts select males for breeding based on such characteristics because they indicate resistance to parasites and other disease.

## QUANTITATIVE ECOLOGY

When considering the distribution of a single parasite species, one finds that parasite individuals exhibit an aggregated distribution among host individuals. This means that most hosts harbour a few or no parasites, while a few hosts carry the vast majority of parasite individuals. This poses considerable problems for students of parasite ecology: the use of parametric statistics should be avoided. Log-transformation of data before the application of parametric test, or the use of non-parametric statistics is recommended by several authors; however, these give rise to further problems. Therefore, modern day quantitative parasitology is based on more advanced biostatistical methods.

### Diversity Ecology

Hosts represent discrete habitat patches that can be occupied by parasites. A hierarchical set of terminology has come into use to describe parasite assemblages at different host scales.

An infrapopulation is all the parasites of one species in a single individual host.

A metapopulation is all the parasites of one species in a host population.

An infracommunity is all the parasites of all species in a single individual host.

A component community is all the parasites of all species in a host population.

A compound community is all the parasites of all species in all host species in an ecosystem.

The diversity ecology of parasites differs markedly from that of free-living organisms. That is, the determinants of species richness and relative abundance animals. For free-living organisms, diversity ecology features many strong conceptual frameworks including Macarthur and Wilson's theory of island biogeography, Diamond's assembly rules and, more recently, null models such as Hubbell's neutral theory of biodiversity and biogeography. Frameworks are not so well-developed for parasites and in many ways they do not fit the free-living models. For example, island biogeography is predicated on fixed spatial relationships between habitat patches ("sinks"), usually with reference to a mainland ("source"). Parasites inhabit hosts, which represent mobile habitat patches with dynamic spatial relationships. There is no true "mainland" other than the sum of hosts (host population); in this way, parasite component communities in host populations are metacommunities.

Nonetheless, different types of parasite assemblages have been recognised in host individuals and populations, and many of the patterns observed for free-living organisms are also pervasive among parasite assemblages. The most prominent of these is the interactive-isolationist continuum. This proposes that parasite assemblages occur along a cline from interactive communities, where niches are saturated and interspecific competition is high, to isolationist communities, where there are many vacant niches and interspecific interaction is not as important as stochastic factors in providing structure to the community. Whether this is so, or whether community patterns simply reflect the sum of underlying species distributions (no real "structure" to the community), has not yet been established.

## ADAPTATION

Parasites are more effective in infecting the hosts they exist with in the same geographical area (sympatric). This effectiveness of the parasites is supported by the "Red Queen hypothesis - which states that interactions between species (such as host an parasites) lead to constant natural selection for adaptation and counter adaptation." The parasites track the locally common host genotypes which help them to adapt to their hosts. On the contrary, the parasites are less infective to allopatric (from different geographical region) hosts. In one of the experiments, two sample of snails were takes from two sources- lake Lanthe and lake Poerua in New Zealand. Also the sample of parasites (digenetic trematode) was taken from each lake. The snails were infected by their sympatric and allopatric parasites and finally they were infected by mixed source of parasites. In the results, it was observed that the parasites were highly effective in infecting the sympatric host than allopatric hosts. However, allopatric hosts also got infected on a very small scale. Hence, the parasite was found to be adapted to infecting local populations of its snail hosts

## TRANSMISSION

Parasites inhabit living organisms, and as a result face problems that free-living organisms do not. Hosts, the only habitats in which parasites can survive, actively try to avoid, repel and destroy parasites. Parasites employ numerous strategies for getting from one host to another, a process sometimes referred to as parasite transmission, or the colonization of new hosts.

Many endoparasites infect their host by penetrating its external surface, while others must be ingested by the host. Once inside the host, adult endoparasites need to shed offspring into the external environment in order to infect other hosts. Many adult endoparasites reside in the host's gastrointestinal tract, where offspring can be shed along with host excreta. Adult stages of tapeworms, thorny-headed worms and most flukes use this method.

Among protozoan endoparasites, such as the malarial parasites and trypanosomes, infective stages in the host's blood are transported to new hosts by biting-insects, or vectors.

Larval stages of endoparasites often infect sites in the host other than the blood or gastrointestinal tract. In many such cases, larval endoparasites require their host to be consumed by the next host in the parasite's life cycle in order to survive and reproduce. Alternatively, larval endoparasites may shed free-living transmission stages that migrate through the host's tissue into the external environment, where they actively search for or await ingestion by other hosts. The foregoing strategies are used, variously, by larval stages of tapeworms, thorny-headed worms, flukes and parasitic roundworms.

Many ectoparasites, such as monogenean worms, rely on direct contact between hosts to colonize new hosts, but other methods are also used. Ectoparasitic arthropods may rely on host-host contact (e.g. many lice) shed eggs that survive off the host (e.g. fleas) and/or wait in the external environment for an encounter with a host (e.g. ticks). Some aquatic leeches locate hosts by sensing movement and only attach when certain temperature and chemical cues are present.

Some parasites modify host behaviour to make transmission to other hosts more likely. For example, in California salt marshes, the fluke *Euhaplorchis californiensis* reduces the ability of its killifish host to avoid predators This parasite matures in egrets, which are more likely to feed on infected killifish than on uninfected fish. Another example is the protozoan *Toxoplasma gondii*, a parasite that matures in cats but can be carried by many other mammals. Uninfected rats avoid cat odours, but rats infected with *T. gondii* are drawn to this scent, a change which may increase transmission to feline hosts.

**Roles in Ecosystems**

Modifying the behaviour of infected hosts to make transmission to other hosts more likely is one way parasites can affect the structure of ecosystems. For example, in the case of *Euhaplorchis californiensis*, discussed above, it is plausible that the abundance of local predator and prey species would be different if this parasite were absent from the system.

Although parasites are often omitted in depictions of food webs, they usually occupy the top position. Parasites can function like keystone species, reducing the dominance of superior competitors and allowing competing species to co-exist.

Many parasites require multiple hosts of different species to complete their life cycles and rely on predator-prey or other stable ecological interactions to get from one host to another. In this sense, the parasites in an ecosystem reflect the "health" of that system.

## CESTODA

Cestoda is a class of parasitic flatworms, commonly called tapeworms, that live in the digestive tract of vertebrates as adults and often in the bodies of various animals as juveniles. *Taenia saginata*, the beef tapeworm, can grow up to 40 feet long (12 m); other species may grow to over 100 feet (30 m).

### Overview

Craig and Ito describe the gut-dwelling worm as segmented and band-like in its adult stage Its first stage in tissues and organs of vertebrates, including humans, is the growth of a cyst-like juvenile (or metacestode). The potential cause of illness and disease is due to a metacestode stage happening in human tissues, rather than an adult tapeworm.

The tegument is the body surface of the adult tapeworm. Tapeworms take the host's nutrients and do not attack the mucosa of the small intestine or remove blood. Infections, therefore, are benign. Most often hosts do not show any signs of illness. A carrier can notice the segments (*proglottides*) when using the bathroom, for instance, in the feces in a toilet bowl. Because tapeworms move around constantly, one may find them in undergarments.

## SCOLEX

The worm's *scolex* ("head") attaches to the intestine of the definitive host. In some species, the scolex is dominated by bothria, which are sometimes called "sucking grooves", and function like suction cups. Other species have hooks and suckers that aid in attachment. Cyclophyllid cestodes can be identified by the presence of four suckers on their scolex, though they may have other structures.

While the scolex is often the most distinctive part of an adult tapeworm, it is often unnoticed in a clinical setting as it is inside the patient. Thus, identifying eggs and proglottids in feces is important.

### Muscular System

The main nerve center of a cestode is in its scolex. Motor and sensory innervation depends on the number and complexity of the scolex. Smaller nerves emanate from the commissures to supply the general body muscular and sensory ending. The cirrus and vagina are innervated and sensory endings around the genital pore are more plentiful than other areas. Sensory function includes both tactoreception and chemoreception.

**Proglottids**

The body is composed of successive segments (*proglottids*). The sum of the proglottids is called a strobila, which is thin, resembling a strip of tape, and is the source of the common name "tapeworm". Like some other flatworms, cestodes use flame cells (protonephridia) for excretion, which are located in the proglottids.

Mature or gravid proglottids are released from the tapeworm and leave the host in its feces.

Because each proglottid contains the male and female reproductive structures, they can reproduce independently. It has been suggested by some biologists that each should be considered a single organism, and that the tapeworm is actually a colony of proglottids.

The layout of proglottids comes in two forms, craspedote, meaning proglottids are overlapped by the previous proglottid, and acraspedote which indicates a non-overlapping conjoined proglottid.

**PARASITIC WORMS**

These can be categorized into three groups; cestodes, nematodes and trematodes. Examples include:

- Acanthocephala
- Ascariasis (roundworms)
- Cestoda (tapeworms) including: *Taenia saginata* (human beef tapeworm), *Taenia solium* (human pork tapeworm), *Diphyllobothrium latum* (fish tapeworm) and Echinococcosis (hydatid tapeworm)
- *Clonorchis sinensis* (the Chinese liver fluke)
- *Dracunculus medinensis* (Guinea Worm)

- *Enterobius vermicularis* (pinworm)
- Filariasis
- Hookworm
- Loa loa
- Onchocerciasis (river blindness)
- Schistosomiasis
- *Strongyloides stercoralis*
- *Toxocara canis* (dog roundworm)
- Trichinella
- Whipworm
- pop soli- a worm to receive blood from humans

**Fungi**

- Ringworm
- Gymnosporangium and other rusts
- Pyrenophora teres
- Cordyceps

**Protists (Protozoa)**

- *Balantidium coli* (the only ciliated protozoan to infect humans)
- *Giardia lamblia* (the most common intestinal protozoan in the United States)
- *Trichomonas vaginalis*
- *Naegleria fowleri* (facultative parasite causing amoebic meningitis)
- *Entamoeba histolytica* (causes Amebiasis, common in developing countries)
- Kinetoplastid protists of the *Trypanosoma* and *Leishmania* genera (sleeping sickness, Chagas disease and leishmania)

- Apicomplexan parasites including "Plasmodium" (malaria), "Toxoplasma" (toxoplasmosis), and "Cryptosporidia" (cryptosporidiosis)

**Ectoparasites**

*ecto* = outside; parasites that live on but not within their hosts, for example, attached to their skin.

**Plants**

- Broomrape
- Cuscuta
- Mistletoe
- Strangler Fig
- Santalum, hemi-parasitic. (Sandalwoods and Quandongs)
- Toothwort
- The wood rose, *Dactylanthus taylorii*

**Arthropoda**

- Acarina (Ticks, some mites)
- Varroa destructor
- *Cymothoa exigua*
- Hippoboscoidea
- Tsetse fly
- Lipoptena
- Sheep Keds and relatives)
- Oestridae (bot flies)
- Human botfly
- Phthiraptera (Lice)
- Body louse
- Crab louse
- Head louse

- Siphonaptera (Fleas)
- Tantulocarida

**Annelids**

- Hirudinea (some leeches)

**Vertebrates**

- Candiru (Vampire fish of Brazil, really a facultative parasite)
- Lampreys

## PARASITIC PLANT

A parasitic plant is one that derives some or all of its sustenance from another plant. About 4,100 species in approximately 19 families of flowering plants are known. Parasitic plants have a modified root, the haustorium, that penetrates the host plant and connects to the xylem, phloem, or both. Parasitic plants are characterized as follows:

1a. Obligate parasite – a parasite that cannot complete its life cycle without a host.

1b. Facultative parasite – a parasite that can complete its life cycle independent of a host.

2a. Stem parasite – a parasite that attaches to the host stem.

2b. Root parasite – a parasite that attaches to the host root.

3a. Holoparasite – a plant that is completely parasitic on other plants and has virtually no chlorophyll.

3b. Hemiparasite – a plant that is parasitic under natural conditions and is also photosynthetic to some degree. Hemiparasites may just obtain water and mineral nutrients from the host plant. Many obtain at least part of their organic nutrients from the host as well.

For hemiparasites, one from each of the three sets of terms can be applied to the same species, e.g.

- *Nuytsia floribunda* is an obligate root hemiparasite.
- *Rhinanthus* (Yellow rattle) is a facultative root hemiparasite.

- Mistletoe is an obligate stem hemiparasite.

Holoparasites are always obligate so only two terms are needed, e.g.

- Dodder is a stem holoparasite.
- *Hydnora* spp. are root holoparasites.

Plants usually considered holoparasites include broomrape, dodder, *Rafflesia*, and Hydnoraceae. Plants usually considered hemiparasites include *Castilleja*, mistletoe, Western Australian Christmas tree and yellow rattle.

**Host Range**

Some parasitic plants are generalists and parasitize many different species, even several different species at once. Dodder (*Cuscuta* sp., *Cassytha* sp.) and red rattle (*Odontites verna*) are generalist parasites. Other parasitic plants are specialists that parasitize a few or even just one species. Beech drops (*Epifagus virginiana*) is a root holoparasite only on American Beech (*Fagus grandifolia*). *Rafflesia* is a holoparasite on the vine *Tetrastigma*.

**Importance**

- Witchweed, broomrape and dodder cause huge economic losses in a variety of herbaceous crops. Mistletoes cause economic damage to forest and ornamental trees.
- *Rafflesia arnoldii* produces the world's largest flowers at about one meter in diameter. It is a tourist attraction in its native habitat.
- Indian paintbrush (*Castilleja linariaefolia*) is the state flower of Wyoming.
- The Oak Mistletoe (*Phoradendron serotinum*) is the state flower of Oklahoma.
- A few other parasitic plants are occasionally cultivated for their attractive flowers, such as *Nutysia* and broomrape.
- Parasitic plants are important in research, especially on the loss of photosynthesis during evolution.

- A few dozen parasitic plants have occasionally been used as food by people.
- Western Australian Christmas tree (*Nuytsia floribunda*) sometimes damages underground cables. It mistakes the cables for host roots and tries to parasitize them using its sclerenchymatic guillotine.

## Myco-heterotrophy

Myco-heterotrophy is a symbiotic relationship between certain kinds of plants and fungi, in which the plant gets all or part of its food from parasitism upon fungi rather than from photosynthesis. A myco-heterotroph is the parasitic plant partner in this relationship. Myco-heterotrophy is considered a kind of cheating relationship and myco-heterotrophs are sometimes informally referred to as "mycorrhizal cheaters". This relationship is sometimes referred to as mycotrophy, though this term is also used for plants that engage in mutualistic mycorrhizal relationships.

### Relationship Between Myco-heterotrophs and Host Fungi

Full (or obligate) myco-heterotrophy exists when a non-photosynthetic plant (a plant largely lacking in chlorophyll or otherwise lacking a functional photosystem) gets all of its food from the fungi that it parasitizes. Partial (or facultative) myco-heterotrophy exists when a plant is capable of photosynthesis, but parasitizes fungi as a supplementary food supply. There are also plants, such as some orchid species, that are non-photosynthetic and obligately myco-heterotrophic for part of their life cycle, and photosynthetic and facultatively myco-heterotrophic or non-myco-heterotrophic for the rest of their life cycle (Not all non-photosynthetic or "achlorophyllous" plants are myco-heterotrophic – some non-photosynthetic plants like dodder directly parasitize the vascular tissue of other plants.

In the past, non-photosynthetic plants were mistakenly thought to get food by breaking down organic matter in a manner similar to saprotrophic fungi. Such plants were therefore called "saprophytes". It is now known that no plant is physiologically capable of direct breakdown of organic matter and that in order to get food, non-photosynthetic plants must engage in parasitism, either through myco-heterotrophy or direct parasitism of other plants.

The interface between the plant and fungal partners in this association is between the roots of the plant and the mycelium of the fungus. Myco-heterotrophy therefore closely resembles mycorrhiza (and indeed is thought to have evolved from mycorrhiza), except that in myco-heterotrophy, the flow of carbon is from the fungus to the plant, rather than vice versa.

Myco-heterotrophs can therefore be seen as ultimately being epiparasites, since they take energy from fungi that in turn get their energy from vascular plants. Indeed, much myco-heterotrophy takes place in the context of a common mycorrhizal network, in which plants use mycorrhizal fungi to exchange carbon and nutrients with other plants. n these systems, myco-heterotrophs play the role of "mycorrhizal cheaters", taking carbon from the common network, but giving nothing in return.

**Species Diversity of Myco-heterotrophs and Host Fungi**

Myco-heterotrophs are found among a number of plant groups. All monotropes and non-photosynthetic orchids are full myco-heterotrophs, as is the non-photosynthetic liverwort *Cryptothallus*. Partial myco-heterotrophy is common in the Gentian family, in photosynthetic orchids, and a number of other plant groups. Some ferns and clubmosses have myco-heterotrophic gametophyte stages The fungi that are parasitized by myco-heterotrophs are typically fungi with large energy reserves to draw on, usually mycorrhizal fungi, though there is some evidence that they may also parasitize parasitic fungi that form extensive mycelial networks, such as *Armillaria*.

# Chapter–11

# Fungus as Protists

## INTRODUCTION

Afungus is a eukaryotic organism that is a member of the kingdom Fungi. The fungi are heterotrophic organisms possessing a chitinous cell wall. The majority of species grow as multicellular filaments called hyphae forming a mycelium; some fungal species also grow as single cells. Sexual and asexual reproduction of the fungi is commonly via spores, often produced on specialized structures or in fruiting bodies. Some species have lost the ability to form reproductive structures, and propagate solely by vegetative growth. Yeasts, molds, and mushrooms are examples of fungi. The fungi are a monophyletic group that is phylogenetically clearly distinct from the morphologically similar slime molds (myxomycetes) and water molds (oomycetes). The fungi are more closely related to animals than plants, yet the discipline of biology devoted to the study of fungi, known as mycology, often falls under a branch of botany.

Occurring worldwide, most fungi are largely invisible to the naked eye, living for the most part in soil, dead matter, and as symbionts of plants, animals, or other fungi. They perform an essential role in all ecosystems in decomposing organic matter and are indispensable in nutrient cycling and exchange. Some fungi become noticeable when fruiting, either as mushrooms or molds. Many fungal species have long been used as a direct source of food, such as mushrooms and truffles and in fermentation of various food products, such as wine, beer, and soy sauce. More recently, fungi are being used as sources for antibiotics used in medicine and various enzymes, such as cellulases, pectinases, and proteases, important for industrial use or as active ingredients of detergents. Many fungi produce bioactive compounds called mycotoxins, such as alkaloids and polyketides that are toxic to animals including humans. Some fungi are used recreationally or in traditional ceremonies as a source of psychotropic compounds. Several species of the fungi are significant pathogens of humans and other animals, and losses due to diseases of crops (e.g., rice blast disease) or food spoilage caused by fungi can have a large impact on human food supply and local economies.

## ETYMOLOGY AND DEFINITION

The English word *fungus* is directly adopted from the Latin *fungus*, meaning "mushroom", used in Horace and Pliny. This in turn is derived from the Greek word *sphongos* ("sponge"), referring to the macroscopic structures and morphology of some mushrooms and molds and also used in other languages (e.g., the German *Schwamm* ("sponge") or *Schwammerl* for some types of mushroom).

### Diversity

Fungi have a worldwide distribution, and grow in a wide range of habitats, including deserts. Most fungi grow in terrestrial environments, but several species occur only in aquatic habitats. Fungi along with bacteria are the primary decomposers of organic matter in most if not all terrestrial ecosystems worldwide. Based on observations of the ratio of the number of fungal species to the number of plant species in some environments, the fungal kingdom has been estimated to contain about 1.5 million species. Around 70,000 fungal species have been formally described by taxonomists, but the true dimension of fungal diversity is still unknown. most fungi grow as thread-like filaments called hyphae, which form a mycelium, while others grow as single cells. Until recently many fungal species were described based mainly on morphological characteristics, such as the size and shape of spores or fruiting structures, and biological species concepts; the application of molecular tools, such as DNA sequencing, to study fungal diversity has greatly enhanced the resolution and added robustness to estimates of diversity within various taxonomic groups.

## IMPORTANCE FOR HUMAN USE

Human use of fungi for food preparation or preservation and other purposes is extensive and has a long history: yeasts are required for fermentation of beer, wine and bread, some other fungal species are used in the production of soy sauce and tempeh. Mushroom farming and mushroom gathering are large industries in many countries. Many fungi are producers of antibiotics, including ß-lactam antibiotics such as penicillin and cephalosporin. Widespread use of these antibiotics for the treatment of bacterial diseases, such as tuberculosis, syphilis, leprosy, and many others began in the early 20th century and continues to play a major part in anti-bacterial chemotherapy. The study of the historical uses and sociological impact of fungi is known as ethnomycology.

### Cultured Foods

Baker's yeast or *Saccharomyces cerevisiae*, a single-cell fungus, is used in the baking of bread and other wheat-based products, such as pizza and dumplings. Several yeast species of the genus Saccharomyces are also used in the production of alcoholic beverages through fermentation. Mycelial fungi, such as the shoyu koji mold (*Aspergillus oryzae*), are used in the brewing of Shoyu (soy sauce) and preparation of tempeh Quorn is a high-protein product made from the mold, *Fusarium venenatum*, and is used in vegetarian cooking.

### Other Human Uses

Fungi are also used extensively to produce industrial chemicals like lactic acid, antibiotics and even to make stonewashed jeans. Several fungal species are ingested for their psychedelic properties, both recreationally and religiously (see main article, *Psilocybin mushrooms*).

## MYCOTOXINS

Many fungi produce compounds with biological activity. Several of these compounds are toxic and are therefore called mycotoxins, referring to their fungal origin and toxic activity. Of particular relevance to humans are those mycotoxins that are produced by moulds causing food spoilage and poisonous mushrooms (see below). Particularly infamous are the aflatoxins, which are insidious liver toxins and highly carcinogenic metabolites produced by *Aspergillus* species often growing in or on grains and nuts consumed by humans, and the lethal amatoxins produced by mushrooms of the genus *Amanita*. Other notable mycotoxins include ochratoxins, patulin, ergot alkaloids, and trichothecenes and fumonisins, all of which have significant impact on human food supplies or animal livestock.

Mycotoxins belong to the group of secondary metabolites (or natural products). Originally, this group of compounds had been thought to be mere byproducts of primary metabolism, hence the name "secondary" metabolites. However, recent research has shown the existence of biochemical pathways solely for the purpose of producing mycotoxins and other natural products in fungi. Mycotoxins provide a number of fitness benefits to the fungi that produce them in terms of physiological adaptation, competition with other microbes and fungi, and protection from fungivory. These fitness benefits and the existence of dedicated biosynthetic pathways for mycotoxin production suggest that the mycotoxins are important for fungal persistence and survival.

## EDIBLE AND POISONOUS FUNGI

Some of the best known types of fungi are the edible and the poisonous mushrooms. Many species are commercially raised, but others must be harvested from the wild. *Agaricus bisporus*, sold as button mushrooms when small or Portobello mushrooms when larger, are the most commonly eaten species, used in salads, soups, and many other dishes. Many Asian fungi are commercially grown and have gained in popularity in the West. They are often available fresh in grocery stores and markets, including straw mushrooms (*Volvariella volvacea*), oyster mushrooms (*Pleurotus ostreatus*), shiitakes (*Lentinula edodes*), and enokitake (*Flammulina* sp.).

There are many more mushroom species that are harvested from the wild for personal consumption or commercial sale. Milk mushrooms, morels, chanterelles, truffles, black trumpets, and *porcini* mushrooms (*Boletus edulis*) (also known as king boletes) all demand a high price on the market. They are often used in gourmet dishes.

For certain types of cheeses, it is also a common practice to inoculate milk curds with fungal spores to foment the growth of specific species of mold that impart a unique flavor and texture to the cheese. This accounts for the blue colour in cheeses such as Stilton or Roquefort which is created using *Penicillium roqueforti* spores Molds used in cheese production are usually non-toxic and are thus safe for human consumption; however, mycotoxins (e.g., aflatoxins, roquefortine C, patulin, or others) may accumulate due to fungal spoilage during cheese ripening or storage.

Many mushroom species are toxic to humans, with toxicities ranging from slight digestive problems or allergic reactions as well as hallucinations to severe organ failures and death. Some of the most deadly mushrooms belong to the genera *Inocybe*, *Cortinarius*, and most infamously, *Amanita*. The latter genus includes the destroying angel *(A. virosa)* and the death cap *(A. phalloides)*, the most common cause of deadly mushroom poisoning. The false morel (*Gyromitra esculenta*) is considered a delicacy by some when cooked, yet can be highly toxic when eaten raw. *Tricholoma equestre* was considered edible until being implicated in some serious poisonings causing rhabdomyolysis.

Fly agaric mushrooms (*A. muscaria*) also cause occasional poisonings, mostly as a result of ingestion for use as a recreational drug for its hallucinogenic properties. Historically Fly agaric was used by Celtic Druids in Northern Europe and the Koryak people of north-eastern Siberia for religious or shamanic purposes. It is difficult to identify a safe mushroom without proper training and knowledge, thus it is often advised to assume that a mushroom in the wild is poisonous and not to consume it.

## FUNGI IN THE BIOLOGICAL CONTROL OF PESTS

In agricultural settings, fungi that actively compete for nutrients and space with, and eventually prevail over, pathogenic microorganisms, such as bacteria or other fungi, via the competitive exclusion principle or are parasites of these pathogens, may be beneficial agents for human use. For example, some fungi may be used to suppress growth or eliminate harmful plant pathogens, such as insects, mites, weeds, nematodes and other fungi that cause diseases of important crop plants This has generated strong interest in the use and practical application of these fungi for the biological control of these agricultural pests. Entomopathogenic fungi can be used as biopesticides, as they actively kill insects. Examples of fungi that have been used as biological insecticides are *Beauveria bassiana*, *Metarhizium anisopliae*, *Hirsutella* sp, *Paecilomyces* sp, and *Verticillium lecanii* Endophytic fungi of grasses of the genus *Neotyphodium*, such as *N. coenophialum* produce alkaloids that are toxic to a range of invertebrate and vertebrate herbivores. These alkaloids protect the infected grass plants from herbivory, but some endophyte alkaloids can cause poisoning of grazing animals, such as cattle and sheep. Infection of grass cultivars of turf or forage grasses with isolates of the grass endophytes that produce only specific alkaloids to improve grass hardiness and resistance to herbivores such as insects, while being non-toxic to livestock, is being used in grass breeding programmes.

### Bioremediation

Certain fungi, in particular 'white rot' fungi, can degrade insecticides, herbicides, pentachlorophenol, creosote, coal tars, and heavy fuels and turn them into carbon dioxide, water, and basic elements esearch has recently discovered that fungi can be used to lock uranium into mineral form.

# Chapter–12

# Molds

## INTRODUCTION

Molds include all species of microscopic fungi that grow in the form of multicellular filaments, called hyphae In contrast, microscopic fungi that grow as single cells are called yeasts. A connected network of these tubular branching hyphae has multiple, genetically identical nuclei and is considered a single organism, referred to as a colony or in more technical terms a mycelium.

Molds do not form a specific taxonomic or phylogenetic grouping, but can be found in the divisions *Zygomycota, Deuteromycota* and *Ascomycota*. Although some molds cause disease or food spoilage, others are useful for their role in biodegradation or in the production of various foods, beverages, antibiotics and enzymes.

Mold covering a decaying peach over a period of six days. The frames were taken approximately 12 hours apart. There are 12 frames of changes.

Moldy nectarines that were in a refrigerator. The nectarine with black mold is also affecting the nectarine underneath.

There are hundreds of known species of molds, which include opportunistic pathogens, saprotrophs, aquatic species, calders and thermophiles. Like all fungi, molds derive energy not through photosynthesis but from the organic matter, inside of which they live. Typically, molds secrete hydrolytic enzymes, mainly from the hyphal tips. These enzymes degrade complex biopolymers such as starch, cellulose and lignin into simpler substances which can be absorbed by the hyphae. In this way, molds play a major role in causing decomposition of organic material, enabling the recycling of nutrients throughout ecosystems. Many molds also secrete mycotoxins which, together with hydrolytic enzymes, inhibit the growth of competing microorganisms.

Molds reproduce through small spores, which may contain a single nucleus or be multinucleate. Mold spores can be asexual (the products of mitosis) or sexual (the products of meiosis); many species can produce both types. Some can remain airborne indefinitely, and many are able to survive extremes of temperature and pressure.

Although molds grow on dead organic matter everywhere in nature, their presence is only visible to the unaided eye when mold colonies grow. A mold colony does not comprise discrete organisms, but an interconnected network of hyphae called a mycelium. Nutrients and in some cases organelles may be transported throughout the mycelium. In artificial environments like buildings, humidity and temperature are often stable enough to foster the growth of mold colonies, commonly seen as a downy or furry coating growing on food or other surfaces.

Some molds can begin growing at temperatures as low as 2°C. When conditions do not enable growth, molds may remain alive in a dormant state, within a large range of temperatures before they die. The many different mold species vary enormously in their tolerance to temperature and humidity extremes. Certain molds can survive harsh conditions such as the snow-covered soils of Antarctica, refrigeration, highly acidic solvents, and even petroleum products such as jet fuel.

Xerophilic molds use the humidity in the air as their only water source; other molds need more moisture.

**Common Molds**

- Acremonium
- Aspergillus
- Cladosporium
- Fusarium
- Mucor
- Penicillium
- Rhizopus
- Stachybotrys
- Trichoderma

**Uses**

Food Production

Cultured molds are used in the production of foods, including:

- cheese (*Penicillium* spp.)
- tempeh (*Rhizopus oligosporus*)
- Quorn (*Fusarium venenatum*)
- sausages
- soy sauce

The *koji* molds are a group of *Aspergillus* species, notably *Aspergillus oryzae,* that have been cultured in eastern Asia for many centuries. They are used to ferment a soybean and wheat mixture to make soybean paste and soy sauce. They are also used to break down the starch in rice (saccharification) in the production of *sake* and other distilled spirits.

**Drug Creation**

Alexander Fleming's famous discovery of the antibiotic penicillin involved the mold *Penicillium chrysogenum*.

Several cholesterol-lowering drugs (such as Lovastatin, from *Aspergillus terreus*) are derived from molds.

The immunosuppressant drug cyclosporine, used to suppress the rejection of transplanted organs, is derived from the mold *Tolypocladium inflatum*.

**Other Uses**

Other molds are cultivated for their ability to produce useful substances. *Aspergillus niger* is used in the production of citric acid, gluconic acid and many other compounds and enzymes. The mold *Aspergillus nidulans* is an important model organism. *Ashbya gossypii* is used in industrial production of riboflavin and is further studied as a model organism.

**Health Effects**

Molds are ubiquitous in nature, and mold spores are a common component of household and workplace dust. However, when mold spores are present in large quantities, they can present a health hazard to humans, potentially causing allergic reactions and respiratory problems.

Some molds also produce mycotoxins that can pose serious health risks to humans and animals. Exposure to high levels of mycotoxins can lead to neurological problems and in some cases death. Prolonged exposure, e.g. daily workplace exposure, can be particularly harmful. The term toxic mold refers to molds that produce mycotoxins, such as Stachybotrys chartarum, and not to all molds in general.

**Growth in Buildings and Gomes**

Mold growth in buildings can lead to a variety of health issues. Various practices can be followed to mitigate mold issues in buildings, the most important of which is to reduce moisture levels that can facilitate mold growth. Removal of affected materials after the source of moisture has been reduced and/or eliminated may be necessary for remediation.

**MOLD MITE**

Mold mites is a general term that refers to a variety of mites (e.g. members of the families Acaridae, Pyroglyphidae, Tarsonemidae) found in association with fungal growths such as mildew, moldy grain, and spoiled food. Many of these mites also are common in house dust.

Most mold mites feed directly on molds, and typically require microbial growth to develop, but others also eat the substrates supporting fungal growth. Common mold mites include the cheese mite (perhaps the most common being *Tyrophagus putrescentiae*, a member of the Acaridae), the flour mite *Dermatophagoides farinae* (a pyrogylphid mite related to a common house dust mite of temperate regions, *D. dermatophagoides*), and the grain mite *Acarus siro* (Acaridae). In the older literature, mold mites are sometimes called tyroglyphid mites, derived from the obsolete family Tyroglyphidae.

Mold mites are very common but usually go unnoticed except when they become abundant. They can infest stored food and grain and cause tremendous losses although they are more commonly an annoyance and nuisance and not injurious. However, as with house dust mites, the exuviae and feces of dust mites may contribute to the development of atopic asthma, rhinitis, and other allergic reactions such as dermatitis in sensitive individuals. Mold mite populations develop to significant levels only where there are microclimates with sufficient humidity and a substrate that will support fungal growth, e.g. areas with leaky pipes and porous surfaces (e.g. wood, rugs, furniture), poorly sealed windows, attics with leaky roofs, hygroscopic foods, and containers of grains, flour, potatoes, etc. The longer you keep infested foods, the higher the mite populations.

Elimination of mold mites is an unrealistic goal: they are ubiquitous in human habitations and food stuffs and, even if they could be eliminated from a household, would soon reinfest. A more useful approach is to limit their population size by denying them the resources they need to develop: moldy organic matter and high local humidities. Mold mites are very small (typically a half millimeter or less in length) and the surface area to volume ratio applies to them: they find it difficult to retain body moisture. Anything that removes moisture (e.g. cleaning up spills, disposing of moldy food, fixing leaky pipes, increasing ventilation with fans, using air conditioning or central heating) from a home will reduce mold mite populations (as well as dust mites and molds - both of which are important sources of antigens).

## MYCORRHIZA

A mycorrhiza (Greek for *fungus roots* coined by Frank, 1885, typically seen in the plural forms *mycorrhizae* or *mycorrhizas*) is a symbiotic (occasionally weakly pathogenic) association between a fungus and the roots of a plant In a mycorrhizal association the fungus may colonize the roots of a host plant either intracellularly or extracellularly.

This mutualistic association provides the fungus with relatively constant and direct access to mono- or dimeric carbohydrates, such as glucose and sucrose produced by the plant in photosynthesis. The carbohydrates are translocated from their source location (usually leaves) to the root tissues and then to the fungal partners. In return, the plant gains the use of the mycelium's very large surface area to absorb water and mineral nutrients from the soil, thus improving the mineral absorption capabilities of the plant roots. Plant roots alone may be incapable of taking up phosphate ions that are immobilized, for example, in soils with a basic pH. The mycelium of the mycorrhizal fungus can however access these phosphorus sources, and make them available to the plants they colonize. The mechanisms of increased absorption are both physical and chemical. Mycorrhizal mycelia are much smaller in diameter than the smallest root, and can explore a greater volume of soil, providing a larger surface area for absorption. Also, the cell membrane chemistry of fungi is different from that of plants. Mycorrhizae are especially beneficial for the plant partner in nutrient-poor soils.

Mycorrhizal plants are often more resistant to diseases, such as those caused by microbial soil-borne pathogens, and are also more resistant to the effects of drought. These effects are perhaps due to the improved water and mineral uptake in mycorrhizal plants.

Mycorrhizae form a mutualistic relationship with the roots of most plant species (although only a small proportion of all species have been examined, 95% of all plant families are predominantly mycorrhizal).

Plants grown in sterile soils and growth media often perform poorly without the addition of spores or hyphae of mycorrhizal fungi to colonise the plant roots and aid in the uptake of soil mineral nutrients. The absence of mycorrhizal fungi can also slow plant growth in early succession or on degraded landscapes.

### Occurrence of Mycorrhizal Associations

At around 400 million years old, the Rhynie chert contains the earliest fossil assemblage yielding plants preserved in sufficient detail to detect mycorrhizae - and they are indeed observed in the stems of *Aglaophyton major*.

Mycorrhizae are present in 92% of plant families (80% of species), with arbuscular mycorrhizae being the ancestral and predominant form, and indeed the most prevalent symbiotic association found in plants at all The structure of arbuscular mycorrhizae has been highly conserved since their first appearance in the fossil record, with both the development of ectomycorrhizae, and the loss of mycorrhizae, evolving convergently on multiple occasions

## TYPES OF MYCORRHIZA

An ericoid mycorrhizal fungus isolated from *Woollsia pungens*.

Mycorrhizas are commonly divided into *ectomycorrhizas* and *endomycorrhizas*. The two groups are differentiated by the fact that the hyphae of ectomycorrhizal fungi do not penetrate individual cells within the root, while the hyphae of endomycorrhizal fungi penetrate the cell wall and invaginate the cell membrane.

### Endomycorrhiza

Endomycorrhiza are variable and have been further classified as arbuscular, ericoid, arbutoid, monotropoid, and orchid mycorrhizae . Arbuscular mycorrhizas, or AM (formerly known as vesicular-arbuscular mycorrhizas, or VAM), are mycorrhizas whose hyphae enter into the plant cells, producing structures that are either balloon-like (vesicles) or dichotomously-branching invaginations (arbuscules). The fungal hyphae do not in fact penetrate the protoplast (i.e. the interior of the cell), but invaginate the cell membrane. The structure of the arbuscules greatly increases the contact surface area between the hypha and the cell cytoplasm to facilitate the transfer of nutrients between them.

Arbuscular mycorrhizae are formed only by fungi in the division Glomeromycota. Fossil evidence and DNA sequence analysis suggest that this mutualism appeared 400-460 million years ago, when the first plants were colonizing land. Arbuscular mycorrhizas are found in 85% of all plant families, and occur in many crop species The hyphae of arbuscular mycorrhizal fungi produce the glycoprotein glomalin, which may be one of the major stores of carbon in the soil. Arbuscular mycorrhizal fungi have (possibly) been asexual for many millions of years and, unusually, individuals can contain many genetically different nuclei (a phenomenon called heterokaryosis).

Many plants in the order Ericales form ericoid mycorrhizas, while some members of the Ericales form arbutoid and monotropoid mycorrhizas. All orchids are mycoheterotrophic at some stage during their lifecycle and form orchid mycorrhiza with a range of basidiomycete fungi.

**Ectomycorrhiza**

Ectomycorrhizas, or EcM, are typically formed between the roots of woody plants and fungi belonging to the Basidiomycota, Ascomycota, and Zygomycota. Ectomycorrhizas consist of a hyphal sheath, or mantle, covering the root tip and a hartig net of hyphae surrounding the plant cells within the root cortex. In some cases the hyphae may also penetrate the plant cells, in which case the mycorrhiza is called an ectendomycorrhiza. Outside the root, the fungal mycelium forms an extensive network within the soil and leaf litter.

Ectomycorrhizas are found in around 10% of plant families, including members of the birch, dipterocarp, eucalyptus, oak, pine and rose families.

The ectomycorrhizal fungus *Laccaria bicolor* has been found to lure and kill springtails to obtain nitrogen, some of which may then be transferred to the mycorrhizal host plant. In a study by Klironomos and Hart, Eastern White Pine inoculated with *L. bicolor* was able to derive up to 25% of its nitrogen from springtails.

## Glomeromycota

Glomeromycota (informally glomeromycetes) is one of seven currently recognized phyla within the kingdom Fungi, with approximately 200 described species. Members of the Glomeromycota form arbuscular mycorrhizas with the roots or thalli (e.g. in bryophytes) of land plants. *Geosiphon pyriformis* forms an endocytobiotic association with *Nostoc* cyanobacteria. AM formation has not yet been shown for all species. The majority of evidence shows that the Glomeromycota are obligate biotrophs, dependent on symbiosis with land plants (*Nostoc* in the case of *Geosiphon*) for carbon and energy, but there is recent circumstantial evidence that some species may be able to lead an independent existence. The arbuscular mycorrhizal species are terrestrial and widely distributed in soils worldwide where they form symbioses with the roots of the majority of plant species. They can also be found in wetlands, including salt-marshes, and associated with epiphytic plants.

### Reproduction

The Glomeromycota have generally coenocytic (occasionally sparsely septate) mycelia and reproduce asexually through blastic development of the hyphal tip to produce spores (Glomerospores) with diameters of 80-500 μm . In some, complex spores form within a terminal saccule.

### Phylogeny

Initial studies of the Glomeromycota were based on the morphology of soil-borne sporocarps (spore clusters) found in or near colonized plant roots Distinguishing features such as wall morphologies, size, shape, colour, hyphal attachment and reaction to staining compounds allowed a phylogeny to be constructed Superficial similarities led to the initial placement of genus *Glomus* in the unrelated family Endogonaceae. Following broader reviews that cleared up the sporocarp confusion, the Glomeromycota were first proposed in the genera *Acaulospora* and *Gigaspora* efore being accorded their own order with the three families Glomaceae (now Glomeraceae), Acaulosporaceae and Gigasporaceae.

With the advent of molecular techniques this classification has undergone major revision. An analysis of small subunit (SSU) rRNA sequences indicated that they share a common ancestor with the Dikarya.

Several species which produce glomoid spores (i.e. spores similar to *Glomus*) in fact belong to other deeply divergent lineages and were placed in the orders, Paraglomerales and Archaeosporales This new classification includes the Geosiphonaceae, which presently contains one fungus (*Geosiphon pyriformis*) that forms endosymbiotic associations with the cyanobacterium *Nostoc punctiforme* and produces spores typical to this phylum, in the Archaeosporales.

Work in this field is incomplete, and members of *Glomus* may be better suited to different genera families

**Molecular Biology**

The biochemical and genetic characterization of the Glomeromycota has been hindered by their biotrophic nature, which impedes laboratory culturing. This obstacle was eventually surpassed with the use of root cultures. The first mycorrhizal gene to be sequenced was the small-subunit ribosomal RNA (SSU rRNA). This gene is highly conserved and commonly used in phylogenetic studies so was isolated from spores of each taxonomic group before amplification through the polymerase chain reaction (PCR). A molecular clock approach, based on the substitution rates of SSU sequences, was used to estimate the time of divergence of the fungi. The molecular analysis found that they are between 462 and 353 Million years old. The data enforces the long-held theory that they were instrumental in the colonization of land by plants.

**Basidiomycota**

Basidiomycota is one of two large phyla that, together with the Ascomycota, comprise the subkingdom Dikarya, which were in general what were called the "Higher Fungi" within the Kingdom Fungi. More specifically the Basidiomycota include mushrooms, puffballs, stinkhorns, bracket fungi, other polypores, jelly fungi, boletes, chanterelles, earth stars, smuts, bunts, rusts, mirror yeasts, and the human pathogenic yeast, *Cryptococcus*. Basically, Basidiomycota are filamentous fungi composed of hyphae (except for those forming yeasts), and reproducing sexually via the formation of specialized club-shaped end cells called basidia that normally bear external spores (usually four), which are specialized meiospores called basidiospores. However, some Basidiomycota reproduce asexually, and may or may not also reproduce sexually. Asexually reproducing Basidiomycota can be recognized as members of this phylum by gross similarity to others, by the formation of a distinctive anatomical feature, cell wall components, and definitively by phylogenetic molecular analysis of DNA sequence data.

**Classification**

The most recent classification adopted by a coalition of 67 mycologists recognizes 3 subphyla (Pucciniomycotina, Ustilaginomycotina, Agaricomycotina) and 2 other class level taxa (Wallemiomycetes, Entorrhizomycetes) outside of these, among the Basidiomycota. As now classified, the subphyla join and also cut across various obsolete taxonomic groups previously commonly used to describe various Basidiomycota.

The Basidiomycota had traditionally been divided into two obsolete classes, the Homobasidiomycetes (including true mushrooms); and the Heterobasidiomycetes (the Jelly, Rust and Smut fungi). Previously the entire Basidiomycota were called Basidiomycetes, an invalid class level name coined in 1959 as a counterpart to the Ascomycetes, when neither of these taxa were recognized as phyla. The terms basidiomycetes and ascomycetes are frequently used loosely to refer to Basidiomycota and Ascomycota. They are often abbreviated to "basidios" and "ascos" as mycological slang.

The Agaricomycotina includes what had previously been called the Hymenomycetes (an obsolete morphological based class of Basidiomycota that formed hymenial layers on their fruitbodies), the Gasteromycetes (another obsolete class that included species mostly lacking hymenia and mostly forming spores in enclosed fruitbodies), as well as most of the jelly fungi.

The Ustilaginomycotina are most (but not all) of the former smut fungi and along with the Exobasidiales.

The Pucciniomycotina includes the rust fungi, the insect parasitic/symbiotic genus *Septobasidium*, a former group of smut fungi (in the Microbotryomycetes, which includes mirror yeasts), and a mixture of odd, infrequently seen or seldom recognized fungi, often parasitic on plants.

Two classes, Wallemiomycetes and Entorrhizomycetes cannot at present be placed in a subphylum.

**Typical Life-cycle**

Unlike higher animals and plants which have readily recognizable male and female counterparts, Basidiomycota [except for the Rust (Pucciniales)] tend to have mutually indistinguishable, compatible haploids which are usually mycelia being composed of filamentous hyphae. Typically haploid Basidiomycota mycelia fuse via plasmogamy and then the compatible nuclei migrate into each other's mycelia and pair up with the resident nuclei. Karyogamy is delayed, so that the compatible nuclei remain in pairs, called a dikaryon. The hyphae are then said to be dikaryotic. Conversely, the haploid mycelia are called monokaryons. Often, the dikaryotic mycelium is more vigorous than the individual monokaryotic mycelia, and proceeds to take over the substrate in which they are growing. The dikaryons can be long-lived, lasting years, decades, or centuries. *The monokaryons are neither male nor female*. They have either a bipolar (unifactorial) or a tetrapolar (bifactorial) mating system. This results in the fact that following meiosis, the resulting haploid basidiospores and resultant monokaryons, have nuclei that are compatible with 50% (if bipolar) or 25% (if tetrapolar) of their sister basidiospores (and their resultant monokaryons) because the mating genes must differ for them to be compatible. However, there are many variations of these genes in the population, and therefore, over 90% of monokaryons are compatible with each other. It is as if there were multiple sexes.

The maintenance of the dikaryotic status in dikaryons in many Basidiomycota is facilitated by the formation of clamp connections that physically appear to help coordinate and re-establish pairs of compatible nuclei following synchronous mitotic nuclear divisions. Variations are frequent and multiple. In a typical Basidiomycota lifecycle the long lasting dikaryons periodically (seasonally or occasionally) produce basidia, the specialized usually club-shaped end cells, in which a pair of compatible nuclei fuse (karyogamy) to form a diploid cell. Meiosis follows shortly with the production of 4 haploid nuclei that migrate into 4 external, usually apical basidiospores. Variations occur, however. Typically the basidiospores are ballistic, hence they are sometimes also called ballistospores. In most species, the basidiospores disperse and each can start a new haploid mycelium, continuing the lifecycle. Basidia are microscopic but they are often produced on or in multicelled large fructifications called basidiocarps or basidiomes, or fruitbodies), variously called mushrooms, puffballs, etc. Ballistic basidiospores are formed on sterigmata which are tapered spine-like projections on basidia, and are typically curved, like the horns of a bull. In some Basidiomycota the spores are not ballistic, and the sterigmata may be straight, reduced to stubbs, or absent. The basidiospores of these non-ballistosporic basidia may either bud off, or be released via dissolution or disintegration of the basidia.

Schematic of a typical basidiocarp, the dipoid reproductive structure of a basidiomycete, showing fruiting body, hymenium and basidia.

In summary, meiosis takes place in a diploid basidium. Each one of the four haploid nuclei migrates into its own basidiospore. The basidiospores are ballistically discharged and start new haploid mycelia called monokaryons. There are no males or females, rather there are compatible thalli with multiple compatibility factors. Plasmogamy between compatible individuals leads to delayed karyogamy leading to establishment of a dikaryon. The dikaryon is long lasting but ultimately gives rise to either fruitbodies with basidia or directly to basidia without fruitbodies. The paired dikaryon in the basidium fuse (i.e karyogamy takes place). The diploid basidium begins the cycle again.

**Variations in Life-cycles**

Many variations occur. Some are self compatible and spontaneously form dikaryons without a separate compatible thallus being involved. These fungi are said to be *homothallic,* versus the normal *heterothallic* species with mating types. Others are secondarily homothallic, in that two compatible nuclei following meiosis migrate into each basidiospore, which is then dispersed as a pre-existing dikaryon. Often such species form only two spores per basidium, but that too varies. Following meiosis, mitotic divisions can occur in the basidium. Multiple numbers of basidiospores can result, including odd numbers via degeneration of nuclei, or pairing up of nuclei, or lack of migration of nuclei. For example, the chanterelle genus *Craterellus* often has 6-spored basidia, while some corticioid *Sistotrema* species can have 2-, 4-, 6-, or 8-spored basidia, and the cultivated button mushroom, *Agaricus bisporus*. can have 1-, 2-, 3- or 4-spored basidia under some circumstances. Occasionally monokaryons of some taxa can form morphologically fully formed basidiomes and anatomically correct basidia and ballistic basidiospores in the absence of dikaryon formation, diploid nuclei, and meiosis. A rare few number of taxa have extended diploid life-cycles, but can be common species. Examples exist in the mushroom genera *Armillaria* and *Xerula,* both in the Physalacriaceae. Occasionally basidiospores are not formed and parts of the "basidia" act as the dispersal agents, e.g. the peculiar mycoparasitic jelly fungus, *Tetragoniomyces* or the entire "basidium" acts as a "spore", e.g. in some false puffballs (*Scleroderma*). In the human pathogenic genus *Filobasidiella* 4 nuclei following meiosis remain in the basidium but continually divide mitotically, each nucleus migrating into synchronously forming nonballistic basidiospores that are then pushed upwards by another set forming below them, resulting in 4 parallel chains of dry "basidiospores".

Other variations occur, some as standard life-cycles (that themselves have variations within variations) within specific orders.

**RUSTS**

Rusts (Pucciniales, previously known as Uredinales) at their greatest complexity produce five different types of spores on two different hosts in two unrelated host families. Such rusts are heteroecious (requiring 2 hosts) and macrocyclic (producing all 5 spores types). Wheat stem rust is an example. By convention the stages and spore states are numbered by Roman numerals. Typically, basidiospores infect host one, the mycelium forms pycnidia, called spermagonia, which are miniature, flask-shaped, hollow, submicroscopic bodies embedded in host tissue (such as a leaf). This stage, numbered "0", produces single-celled, minute spores that ooze out in a sweet liquid and that act as nonmotile spermatia, and also protruding receptive hyphae. Insects and probably other vectors such as rain carry the spermatia from spermagonia to spermagonia, cross inoculating the mating types. Neither thallus is male or female. Once crossed, the dikaryons are established and a second spore stage is formed, numbered "I" and called aecia, which form dikaryotic aeciospores in dry chains in inverted cup-shaped bodies embedded in host tissue. These aeciospores then infect the second host genus and cannot infect the host on which they are formed (in macrocyclic rusts). On the second host a repeating spore stage is formed, numbered "II", the uredospores in dry pustules called uredinia. Urediospores are dikaryotic and can infect the same host that produced them. They repeatedly infect this host over the growing season. At the end of the season, a fourth spore type, the teliospore, is formed. It is thicker-walled and serves to overwinter or to survive other harsh conditions. It does not continue the infection process, rather it remains dormant for a period and then germinates to form basidia (stage "IV"), sometimes called a promycelium. In the Pucciniales, the basidia are cylindrical and become 3-septate after meiosis, with each of the 4 cells bearing one basidiospore each. The basidospores disperse and start the infection process on host 1 again. Autoecious rusts complete their life-cycles on one host intead of two, and microcyclic rusts cut out one or more stages.

## SMUTS

The characteristic part of the life-cycle of smuts is the thick-walled, often darkly pigmented, ornate, teliospore that serves to survive harsh conditions such as overwintering and also serves to help disperse the fungus as dry diaspores. The teliospores are initially dikaryotic but become diploid via karyogamy. Meiosis takes place at the time of germination. A promycelim is formed that consists to a short hypha (equated to a basidium). In some smuts such as *Ustilago maydis* the nuclei migrate into the promycelium that becomes septate, and haploid yeast-like conidia/basidiospores sometimes called sporidia, bud off laterally from each cell. In various smuts, the yeast phase may proliferate, or they may fuse, or they may infect plant tissue and become hyphal. In other smuts, such as *Tilletia caries*, the elongated haploid basidiospores form apically, often in compatible pairs that fuse centrally resulting in "H"-shaped diaspores which are by then dikaryotic. Dikaryotic conidia may then form. Eventually the host is infected by infectious hyphae. Teliospores form in host tissue. Many variations on these general themes occur.

Dimorphic Basidiomycota are smuts with both a yeast phase and an infectious hyphal state are examples of dimorphic Basidiomycota. In plant parasitic taxa, the saprotrophic phase is normally the yeast while the infectious stage is hyphal. However, there are examples of animal and human parasites where the species are dimorphic but it is the yeast-like state that is infectious. The genus *Filobasidiella* forms basidia on hyphae but the main infectious stage is more commonly known by the anamorphic yeast name *Cryptococcus*, e.g. *Cryptococcus neoformans* and *Cryptococcus gattii*.

The dimorphic Basidiomycota with yeast stages and the pleiomorphic rusts are examples of fungi with anamorphs, which are the asexual stages. Some Basidiomycota are only known as anamorphs. Many are yeasts, collectively called basidiomycetous yeasts to differentiate them from ascomycetous yeasts in the Ascomycota. Aside from yeast anamorphs, and uredinia, aecia and pycnidia, some Basidiomycota form other distinctive anamorphs as parts of their life-cycles. Examples are *Collybia tuberosa* with its apple-seed-shaped and coloured sclerotium, *Dendrocollybia racemosa* with its sclerotium and its *Tilachlidiopsis racemosa* conidia, *Armillaria* with their rhizomorphs *Hohenbuehelia* with their *Nematoctonus* nematode infectious, state and the coffee leaf parasite, *Mycena citricolor* and its *Decapitatus flavidus* propagules called gemmae.

## ASCOMYCOTA

Ascomycota is a Division/Phylum of Fungi, and subkingdom Dikarya, whose members are commonly known as the Sac Fungi. Characteristically, when reproducing sexually, they produce nonmotile spores in a distinctive type of microscopic cell called an "ascus" *askos*), meaning "sac" or "wineskin"). These spores are called ascospores. However, some members of the Ascomycota do not reproduce sexually and do not form asci or ascospores. These members are assigned to Ascomycota based upon morphological and/or physiological similarities to ascus-bearing taxa, and in particular by phylogenetic comparisons of DNA sequences.

This monophyletic grouping is an extremely significant and successful group of organisms. Familiar examples of sac fungi include morels, truffles, brewer's yeast and baker's yeast, Dead Man's Fingers, cup fungi, and the majority of lichens (loosely termed "ascolichens") such as *Cladonia*. Many plant-pathogenic fungi belong to the Ascomycota. Commonly seen examples include apple scab, ergot, black knot, and the powdery mildews. Species of ascomycetes are also popular in the laboratory. *Sordaria fimicola*, *Neurospora crassa* and several species of yeasts are used in many genetics and cell biology experiments. *Penicillium* species on cheeses and in the antibiotic industry are examples of asexual taxa, otherwise known as anamorphs, that belong in the Ascomycota. Prior to definitive phylogenetic research, molds such as *Penicillium* were sometimes classified in an artificial phylum, called the Deuteromycota.

### Ascomycetes versus Ascomycota

In the past, before the recognition of the fungal kingdom, the sac fungi were considered to be a *Class*, not a *Phylum*. The original collective term for them was "Ascomycetes", a label first coined in the 1800s for a rankless nonlichenized taxon based upon the presence of asci. "Ascomycetes" was soon used to include lichenized taxa, and became the standard term, at the class level, for all ascus-bearing species, just as the term "Basidiomycetes" became used for their basidium-bearing counterparts. Elevation of the taxonomic rank of the Ascomycetes resulted in the names

Ascomycetae, Ascomycotina, and finally Ascomycota. The names Ascomycota, Ascomycetes, etc. are based upon the term "ascus". Together, the Ascomycota and the Basidiomycota form the subkingdom Dikarya. The more familiar term, Ascomycetes, is still loosely used, e.g. at fungal forays it is often said of a fungus, such as *Peziza*, "It is an ascomycete, not a basidiomycete" in reference to their sexual reproductive mode. The terms are further abbreviated to "ascos" and "basidos" which are not officially sanctioned technical names.

**Modern Classification of Ascomycota**

There are three subphyla that are described and named:

- The subphylum Pezizomycotina is the largest subphylum and contains all the Ascomycota that produce ascocarps (fruiting bodies), except for one genus, *Neolecta*, in the Taphrinomycotina. Therefore, it includes virtually all macroscopic "ascos" such as truffles, ergot, ascolichens, cup fungi (discomycetes), pyrenomycetes, lorchels, and caterpillar fungus as well as many microscopic fungi, e.g. powdery mildews, ring worm fungi, chalkbrood fungus, Laboulbeniales, and most black molds around sinks and tubs. The older named taxon Euascomycetes is roughly equivalent.
- The subphylum Saccharomycotina comprises most of the "true" yeasts, such as baker's yeast and *Candida* which are in general single-celled, or short chains of cells, and reproduce vegetatively by budding rather than by the production of hyphae. As a result, most were classified in a vaguely defined taxon with the older name Hemiascomycetes.
- The subphylum Taphrinomycotina includes a disparate group of Ascomycota and were only recognized as a distinctive group after the advent of molecular DNA) analyses. The group is basal to the other subphyla and hence is considered to be more primitive. Consequently the taxon was originally named Archiascomycetes alternatively spelled Archaeascomycetes. It includes both hyphal fungi *Neolecta, Taphrina*), and fission yeasts *Schizosaccharomyces*

and the peculiar mammalian lung parasite, *Pneumocystis* that was originally believed to be a protozoan.

Evidence from ribosomal RNA gene sequencing of soils indicates that there likely a fourth previously unknown subphylum of Ascomycota (loosely termed Soil Clone Group I - SCGI), that has never been described via cultures or fruitbodies. SCGI organisms are only known from DNA sequences but have been shown to occur in soils worldwide. Placement of this group based on rRNA gene sequencing indicates that they may fall between the Taphriomycotina and the Saccharomycotina, however phenotypic characteristics and environmental roles and significance remain unknown.

## Commonly Used but Obsolete Morphologically Defined Class Names

Several obsolete class names, based upon morphology, are still used in informal or introductory discussions. Among those based upon the sexual fruitbodies (teleomorphs) are: the Discomycetes which included all species forming apothecia; the Pyrenomycetes which included all sac fungi that formed perithecia or even pseudothecia, or any structure approaching these morphological structures; and the Plectomycetes which included those Ascomycota that formed cleistothecia. Hemiascomycetes included the yeasts and yeast-like fungi that are now split between Saccharomycotina and Taphrinomycotina, while the Euascomycetes covered the rest of the Ascomycota, now in the Pezizomycotina and *Neolecta* in the Taphrinomycotina.

Some Ascomycota never reproduce sexually, or are not known to produce asci. These are sometimes called "Mitosporic Ascomycota" because of the production of conidia otherwise known as mitospores, and other asexual structures, all collectively called anamorphic taxa. In some classifications these would have been placed in a separate artificial phylum, the Deuteromycota (also known as Fungi Imperfecti). Molecular analyses can now be used to place these genera and species among ascus-bearing taxa (if they are Ascomycota), or amongst other phyla such as the Basidiomycota (if related to them). No mitosporic taxa have been found that form a phylum distinct from the other major phyla of

Fungi. Anamorphs are discussed below. However, it is extremely difficult in the absence of molecular analysis to link most anamorphic (asexual morphs) fungi to their teleomorphs (sexual counterparts). There are over 250 years of names available (since Linnaeus' Species Plantarum, 1753) for both asexual and sexual components of the same fungi. For instance the sexual form of the kerosene fungus is known as *Amorphotheca resinae* while the asexual stage is called *Hormoconis resinae*. Most anamorphic fungi are Ascomycota, and therefore the obsolete classification of the Deuteromycota is largely that of Ascomycota anamorphs.

The Deuteromycota were classified as Coelomycetes if they produced their conidia in small seed-like, fly-speck sized, flask-shaped conidiomata, or structures resembling or approximating them in structure. The Hyphomycetes were those species where the conidiophores (i.e. the hyphae which carry conidia-forming cells on the end) are free or loosely organized. They are mostly isolated but sometimes also appear as bundles of cells aligned in parallel (described as *synnematal*) or as cushion-shaped masses (described as *sporodochial*).

**Physical Make-up**

The adjective which describes these fungi is "ascomycetous". The majority of ascomycetous fungi grow as a thallus, called a mycelium, consisting of many hyphae which are microscopic multi-branched filaments. If the hyphae of some typical mycelia were laid end to end, they could reach a length of several kilometers. Ascomycota typically produce great numbers of asci at any one time, and these may be contained in a multicellular, often readily visible structure called an "ascocarp" (also called an "ascoma", the fruiting body of ascomycetes). Many exceptions to the structure described above occur, for example in one extreme these fungi are single celled yeasts, and there is no mycelium, no fruitbody, and the entire cell is converted into an ascus in such ascomycetous yeasts such as baker's Yeast (*Saccharomyces cerevisiae*).

In the case of lichenized species, the thallus of the fungus defines the shape of the symbiotic colony. Other Ascomycota are dimorphic, which can mean that they can appear either in single-

or multi-cellular form. Other species are pleomorphic, exhibiting multiple asexual forms (i.e. anamorphs detailed below) as well as a sexual form (a teleomorph). The ascoma come in multiple forms: cup-shaped, club-shaped, potato-like, spongy, seed-like, oozing and pimple-like, coral-like, nit-like, golf-ball-shaped, perforated tennis ball-like, cushion-shaped, plated and feathered in miniature (Laboulbeniales), microscopic classic Greek shield-shaped, stalked or sessile, solitary or clustered, etc. They can be fleshy or carbonaceous (like charcoal), leathery, rubbery, gelatinous, slimy, powdery, or cob-web-like, etc. They come in multiple colours such as red, orange, yellow, and rarely green or blue, although brown or black are more common.

Except for lichens, the mycelium (if produced) is usually inconspicuous because it is subterranean or embedded in the substrate, and only the ascoma is seen in season. But spectacular, bizarre, or otherwise noteworthy exceptions occur. Many ascomatous fungi have melanized hyphal walls (referred to as dematiaceous walls) and therefore are black or brown. Black spots on bathroom caulking are often colonies of Ascomycota, e.g. *Cladosporium*. Many molds that grow on spoiled foods are Ascomycota, and therefore the pellicles or skins that develop on jams, juices, and other foods in containers at home are in fact the thalli of Ascomycota (occasionally Mucorcmycotina, and almost never Basidiomycota). Sooty molds that develop on plants, especially in the tropics are the thalli of many species.

Sometimes it is the mass of asci or ascus-like cells, or conidia or yeast cells that are the conspicuous elements. Pneumocystis species fill lung cavities causing a form of pneumonia (visible in x-rays). Ascosphaera cysts (asci) fill honey bee larvae and pupae making them appear mummified and chalk-like, hence the name "chalkbrood". Free living yeasts form yeast colonies. Excessive *Candida* yeast growth in the mouth or vagina is called "thrush" or candidiasis.

The cell walls of these fungi are almost always formed of Chitin and ß-Glucans; individual cells are formed from divisions of the hyphae called "septa". These give stability to the hyphae and prevent a great loss of cytoplasm in the event that the cell membrane should be locally damaged. Mostly the cell divisions are centrally perforated, so they have a small opening in the middle, through which cytoplasm and also nuclei can move more or less freely throughout the system of hyphae. Often hyphae have only one nucleus per cell, and are therefore described as *uninucleate*, but some ascomycetous fungi can also be multinucleate at times.

**Metabolism**

Like most fungi the Ascomycota principally digest living or dead biomass. To achieve this, they secrete into their surroundings powerful digestive enzymes which break down organic substances into small molecules, which are then absorbed through the cell wall. Many species live on dead plant material such as fallen leaves, twigs, or logs. Others attack plants, animals, or other fungi as parasites and derive their metabolic energy, as well as all the nutrients they need, from the cell tissue of their hosts. Especially in this group extreme specialization appears; for instance certain species of Laboulbeniales attack only one particular leg of one particular insect species. The Ascomycota also often take up symbiotic relationships – for instance some combine with green algae or cyanobacteria, from which they obtain photosynthetic nutrients, to form lichens; others form symbioses with tree roots as mycorrhizal fungi. There are also carnivorous fungi, which have developed hyphal traps in which they can catch small protists such as amoebae, as well as roundworms (*Nematoda*), rotifers, tardigrades, and small arthropods such as springtails (*Collembola*).

Through their long evolutionary history the Ascomycota have developed the capability to break down almost every organic substance. Unlike most organisms they are able to use their own enzymes to digest plant cellulose and the lignin contained in wood. Collagen, an abundant structural protein in animals, and keratin (which hair is made of), can also serve as food sources. Exotic examples are given by the ascomycete *Aureobasidium pullulans*, which metabolizes wall paint, and the kerosene fungus *Amorphotheca resinae*, which (to the misfortune of the airline industry) feeds on aircraft fuel, and in tropical regions sometimes blocks fuel pipes. Others resist osmotic stress to grow on salted fish, and a few live in water.

**Distribution and Living Environment**

The Ascomycota are present in all land ecosystems worldwide – they even occur in Antarctica – and their spores and hyphal fragments are distributed through the atmosphere and fresh water environments, as well as ocean beaches and tidal zones. The distribution of individual species is very variable: some are found on all continents, while for example the white truffle *Tuber magnatum*, which is much sought after for culinary purposes, only appears in isolated locations in Italy and France. Plant parasitic species are often restricted by their host distributions. *Cyttaria* is only found on *Nothofagus* (Southern Beech) in the Southern Hemisphere.

**Asexual Reproduction**

Asexual reproduction is the dominant form of propagation in the Ascomycota, and is responsible for the rapid expansion of these fungi into areas which were previously not colonized. It occurs through reproductive structures, the "conidia," which are genetically identical to the parent and mostly have just one nucleus. They are also called "mitospores" due to the way they are generated through the cellular process of mitosis. They are generally formed on the ends of specialized hyphae, the "conidiophores". Depending on the species they may be dispersed by wind or water, or also by animals.

**Asexual Spores**

In order to further classify the Ascomycota in the asexual stages, it is important to consider the spores, which can be distinguished by colour, form and the way they are separated into cells. The most frequent types are the single-celled spores which are designated *amerospores*. If the spore is divided into two by a

Conidiophores of *Trichoderma fertile* with vase-shaped phialides and newly formed conidia on their ends (bright points) When there are two or more cross-walls the classification depends on the shape. If the septa are *transversal*, like the rungs of a ladder, it is a *phragmospore* whilst if they form a net-like structure it is a *dictyospore*. In *staurospores* ray-like "arms" radiate from a central body; in others (*helicospores*) the entire spore is wound up in a spiral like a spring. Finally very long worm-like spores, of which the ratio length:diameter is more than 15:1, are called *scolecospores*.

**Conidiogenesis and Dehiscence**

One distinguishes:

- acervular conidiomata, or *acervuli*, which develop in the host and can thus be:
  - *subcuticular*, lying under the outer layer of the plant (the cuticle),
  - *intraepidermal*, inside the outer cell layer (the epidermis),
  - *subepidermal*, under the epidermis, or deeper inside the host.

Mostly they develop a flat layer of relatively short conidiophores which then produce masses of spores. The increasing pressure finally leads to the splitting of the epidermis and cuticle and so allows the conidia to escape.

Pycnidial conidiomata or pycnidia, which unlike the acervuli form in the fungal tissue itself, and which are generally shaped like a bulging vase. The spores are released through a small opening at the apex, the ostiole.

Two further important characteristics of the anamorphs of the Ascomycota are the *conidiogenesis*, the fashion in which the spores are formed, and their *dehiscence*, i.e. how they separate from the parent structures. The former corresponds to Embryology in animals and plants and can be divided into two fundamental forms of development: *blastic* conidiogenesis, where the spore is already evident before it separates from the conidiogenic hypha which is giving rise to it, and *thallic* conidiogenesis, where first a cross-wall appears and then the thus created cell develops into a spore.

These two basic types can be further classified as follows.

- *blastic-acropetal* (repeated budding at the tip of the conidiogenic hypha, so that a chain of spores is formed with the youngest at the tip),
- *blastic-synchronous* (simultaneous spore formation from a central cell, sometimes with secondary acropetal chains forming from the initial spores),
- *blastic-sympodial* (repeated sideways spore formation from behind the leading spore, so that the oldest spore is at the main tip),
- *blastic-annellidic* (each spore separates and leaves a ring-shaped scar which is concentrically inside the scar left by the previous spore),
- *blastic-phialidic* (the spores arise and are ejected from the open ends of special conidiogenic cells called phialides which remain constant in length; an example is the anamorph of *Penicillium*),
- *basauxic* (where a chain of conidia, in successively younger stages of development, is emitted from the mother cell),
- *blastic-retrogressive* (spores separate off by formation of crosswalls near the tip of the conidiogenic hypha, which thus becomes progressively shorter),
- *thallic-arthric* (double cell walls split the conidiogenic hypha into cells which develop into short, cylindrical spores called arthroconidia; sometimes every second cell dies off, leaving the arthroconidia free),
- *thallic-solitary* (a large bulging cell separates from the conidiogenic hypha, forms internal walls, and develops to a *phragmospore*).

Essentially dehiscence can happen in two different ways. In the schizolytic variant a double dividing wall with a central lamella (layer) forms *between* the cells; the central layer dissolves to release the spores. In the case of rhexolytic dehiscence on the other hand the cell wall which joins the spores on the *outside* simply degenerates and sets free the conidia.

## HETEROCARYOSIS AND PARASEXUALITY

A significant number of Ascomycota species either have no sexual stage or none is known. In spite of this, there are two ways in which they can conserve their genetic diversity: Heterocaryosis and Parasexuality.

The former happens simply through the merging of two hyphae belonging to different individuals, a process known as anastomosis. As a result there are more cell nuclei than normal in the mycelium and they come from genetically different parent organisms.

Parasexuality, on the other hand, refers to a phenomenon where two cell nuclei merge without any sexual process and the chromosome count is doubled. This involves a complex form of the type of cell division called mitosis, where there is *crossing over* or *recombination*, i.e. an exchange of genetic material between corresponding pairs of chromosomes. In sexual reproduction, in contrast, crossing over occurs only during meiosis. Finally the chromosome count will be restored to normal by haploidization, whereby the nucleus splits into two parts each having a single set of chromosomes, with each daughter genetically different from the original parents.

### Sexual Reproduction

Sexual reproduction in the Ascomycota is marked by a characteristic structure, the *ascus*, which distinguishes these fungi from all others. An ascus is a tube-shaped vessel, a *meiosporangium*, which contains the sexual spores produced by meiosis. The latter are called *ascospores* in contrast to the asexual *conidiospores*.

Apart from exceptions such as baker's Yeast (*Saccharomyces cerevisiae*), almost all fungi of the Ascomycota are haploid, so their nuclei only contain one set of chromosomes, which makes them especially susceptible to mutations. During sexual reproduction there is a diploid phase (with two sets of chromosomes), which as a rule is very short. Then meiosis occurs, generally very soon, so that the haploid state is re-established.

**The Formation of Sexual Spores**

The sexual part of the life cycle commences when two suitable hyphae meet each other. These come from the same web of hyphae which can also generate asexual spores. The first deciding factor as to whether conjugation - that is, sexual merging - will occur, is whether the hyphae belong to the same organism, or whether they come from different individual fungi. Whilst many species are thoroughly capable of self-propagation, i.e. they are homothallic, others need non-identical partners and so are heterothallic. Besides this, the two hyphae in question must also belong to the same mating type. Mating types are a peculiarity of the fungi and correspond roughly to the sexes in plants and animals; however one species may have more than two mating types.

In the case of compatibility, gametangia form on the hyphae; these are the generative cells for the gametes, in which numerous nuclei gather. A very fine hypha, called the trichogyne, which grows out of one gametangium, now termed the ascogonium, makes a passage to a gametangium of the other individual, which is then the antheridium. Nuclei then pass from the antheridium (playing a 'male' role) to the ascogonium (playing a 'female' role).

Unlike the process in animals and plants, after the union of the cytoplasms of the two gametangia (plasmogamy), the merging of the nuclei (karyogamy) does not usually occur immediately. Instead, the nuclei which have migrated in from the antheridium pair up with the nuclei of the ascogonium, but remain separate next to their partners. With this the dikaryophase of the life cycle begins; during this time the pairs of nuclei repeatedly synchronously divide, so that a great number are produced. In all probability the dikaryophase is an evolutionary adaptation which serves to exploit the potential of sexual reproduction to the full in circumstances where it is a rare event for different individuals to meet each other. After the genetic raw material has been increased by repeated division, recombination will take place independently in each pair during meiosis, so that the greatest possible quantity of genetically different spores will arise. In the red algae (Rhodophyta) a similar solution to the corresponding problem evolved independently.

Next millions of new dinucleate hyphae, into each of which two nuclei migrate, emerge from the fertilized ascogonium. They are also called ascogenous or *fertile*. They are fed by ordinary uni- or mononucleate hyphae (with only one nucleus), which are also called *sterile*. The tissue of sterile and fertile hyphae now grows in many cases into a macroscopically visible fruiting body, the ascocarp, which may contain millions of fertile hyphae.

In the actual fruiting layer, the hymenium, the **asci** now appear. At one end of an ascogenous hypha, there develops a U-shaped hook, which points back opposite to the general growth direction. The two nuclei contained in the terminal cell then divide in such a way that the threads of their mitotic spindles run parallel, and thus two pairs of genetically different daughter nuclei arise, with one daughter of each pair near the point of the hook, and the other in the base part of the hypha. Then two parallel cross-walls appear, dividing the hypha into three sections: that at the point of the hook with one nucleus, that at the base of the original hypha with one nucleus, and the middle U-shaped part with two nuclei.

If the positioning in the fruiting layer is right, the karyogamic fusion of the nuclei finally takes place in the U-shaped cell, creating the diploid zygote. It lengthens to form an elongated tube-shaped or cylinder-shaped capsule, the actual ascus. Then meiosis occurs, giving rise to four haploid nuclei. This is almost always followed by a further mitotic division, so that the ascus ultimately has eight daughter nuclei. These become enclosed, together with some of the cell plasma, each by their own membranes, and generally with a hard cell wall. Thus the dissemination cells (the ascospores) develop, lying initially like peas in a pod inside the ascus. Later, when an appropriate opportunity presents itself, they are liberated.

Not having flagella, ascospores are disseminated in various other ways: some are spread by wind and with others the ripe ascus breaks open on contact with water to set free the spores. Certain species have evolved regular 'spore cannons' which can eject them up to 30 cm. away. When the spores reach a suitable substrate, they germinate, form new hyphae, and so restart their life cycle, which has come full circle.

The form of the ascus is important for classification and is divided into four basic types: unitunicate-operculate, unitunicate-inoperculate, bitunicate, or prototunicate. See the article on asci for further details.

The Ascomycota fulfil a central role in most land-based ecosystems. They are important decomposers which break down such organic materials as dead leaves, twigs, fallen trees, etc. and help the detritivores (animals which live off this decomposing material) to obtain their nutrients. By processing substances like cellulose or lignin, which are otherwise difficult to exploit, they take on an important place in the natural nitrogen cycle and the carbon cycle.

Inversely the fruiting bodies of the Ascomycota provide food for a very diverse set of animals from insects and slugs and snails (*Gastropoda*) to rodents and larger mammals such as deer and wild boars.

Fungi of the Ascomycota are also known for their numerous symbiotic relationships with other organisms.

**Lichens**

Cross-section through the lichen *Pseudevernia furfuracea* with plainly visible layer of green algae under the surface

Probably since early in their evolutionary history the Ascomycota have "domesticated" green algae (*Chlorophyta*), as well as occasionally other types of algae and cyanobacteria. Together they form the mutualistic associations known as lichens, which can survive in the least hospitable regions of the earth, including the Arctic, the Antarctic, deserts and mountaintops, and can withstand temperature extremes from -40ºC to +80ºC. While the photoautotrophic algal partner creates metabolic energy through photosynthesis, the fungus offers a stable supportive framework and protects from radiation and drying out. Around 42% of the Ascomycota (numerically about 18,000 species) form lichens, and almost all the fungal partners of lichens belong to the Ascomycota - the proportion of Basidiomycota is probably only two to three per cent.

## Mycorrhizal Fungi and Endophytes

Members of the Ascomycota make two particularly important types of relationship with plants: as mycorrhizal fungi and as endophytes. The former make symbiotic associations with the root systems of the plants, which for some trees, especially conifers, can be of vital importance, enabling the uptake of mineral salts from the soil. The fungal partner is in a much better position to absorb minerals due to its finely divided mycelium, whilst the plant provides it with metabolic energy in the form of photosynthetic products. Cases are even known where mycorrhizal fungi can transport nutrients from one plant to another, stabilizing the recipient. It is likely that mycorrhizal associations enabled the conquest of the land by plants - in any case the earliest known fossils of land plants have mycorrhizae.

Endophytes on the other hand live inside plants, especially in the stem and leaves, but generally do not damage their hosts. The exact nature of the relationship between endophytic fungus and host is not yet well understood, but it seems that this form of colonization can bestow a higher resistance against insects, roundworms (nematodes), and bacteria; also it can enable or augment the production of poisonous alkaloids, chemicals which can affect the health of plant-eating mammals.

A series of Ascomycota species from the genus *Xylaria* are found in the nests of leafcutter ants and other fungus-growing ants of the tribe *Attini* and in the fungal gardens of termites (*Isoptera*). Since they do not generate fruiting bodies until the insects have left the nests, it is suspected that, as confirmed in several cases of Basidiomycota species, they may be cultivated.

On the other hand bark beetles (*Scolytidae*) are certainly important symbiotic partners. The female beetles transport the spores to new hosts in characteristic tucks in their skin, the *mycetangia*. There they eat tunnels in the wood, which lead into large chambers in which they lay their eggs. At this time the spores are released and give rise to hyphae which unlike the beetles can digest the wood. The beetle larvae feed on the fungus and after they have metamorphosed into the adult state they again carry spores with them to renew the cycle of infection. A well-known example of this is Dutch elm disease, caused by fungus *Ophiostoma ulmi*, being carried by the European elm bark beetle *Scolytus multistriatus*.

## Importance for Humans

Ascomycetes make many contributions to the good of humanity, and also have many ill effects.

## Harmful Interactions

One of their most harmful roles is as the agent of many plant diseases. For instance:

- Dutch Elm Disease, caused by the closely related species *Ophiostoma ulmi* and *Ophiostoma novo-ulmi*, has led to the death of many elms in Europe and North America.
- The originally Asian *Cryphonectria parasitica* is responsible for attacking Sweet Chestnuts (*Castanea sativa*), and virtually eliminated the once-widespread American Chestnut (*Castanea dentata*),
- A disease of Maize (*Zea mays*), which is especially prevalent in North America, is brought about by *Cochliobolus heterostrophus*.
- *Taphrina deformans* causes leaf curl of peach.
- *Uncinula necator* is responsible for the disease Powdery mildew, which attacks grapevines.
- Species of *Monilia* cause brown rot of stone fruit such as peaches (*Prunus persica*) and sour cherries (*Prunus ceranus*).
- Members of the Ascomycota such as *Stachybotrys chartarum* are responsible for fading of woollen textiles, which is a common problem especially in the tropics.
- Blue-green, red and brown moulds attack and spoil foodstuffs - for instance *Penicillium italicum* rots oranges.
- Cereals infected with *Fusarium graminearum* contain mycotoxins like deoxynivalenol (DON), which can lead to skin and mucous membrane lesions when eaten by pigs.

- Ergot (*Claviceps purpurea*) is a direct menace to humans when it attacks wheat or rye and produces highly poisonous and carcinogenic alkaloids, causing ergotism if consumed. Symptoms include hallucinations, stomach cramp, and a burning sensation in the limbs ("Saint Anthony's Fire").
- *Aspergillus flavus*, which grows on peanuts and other hosts, generates aflatoxin, which damages the liver and is highly carcinogenic.
- *Candida albicans*, a yeast which attacks the mucous membranes, can cause an infection of the mouth or vagina called thrush or candidiasis, and is also blamed for "yeast allergies".
- Fungi like *Epidermophyton* cause skin infections but are not very dangerous for people with healthy immune systems. However if the immune system is damaged they can be life-threatening; for instance, *Pneumocystis jiroveci* is responsible for severe lung infections which occur in AIDS patients.

**Positive Effects**

On the other hand, ascus fungi have brought some important benefits to humanity.

- The most famous case may be that of the mould *Penicillium chrysogenum* (formerly *Penicillium notatum*), which, probably to attack competing bacteria, produces an antibiotic which, under the name of Penicillin, triggered a revolution in the treatment of bacterial infectious diseases in the 20th century.
- The medical importance of *Tolypocladium niveum* as an immunosuppressor can hardly be exaggerated. It excretes Ciclosporin, which, as well as being given during organ transplants to prevent rejection, is also prescribed for auto-immune diseases such as multiple sclerosis, although there is some doubt over the long-term side-effects of the treatment.

  Stilton cheese veined with *Penicillium roqueforti*

- Some ascomycete fungi can be altered relatively easily through genetic engineering procedures. They can then produce useful proteins such as insulin, human growth hormone, or TPa, which is employed to dissolve blood clots.

- The red bread mould *Neurospora crassa* is an important model organism in biology, of which the genome has now been fully sequenced.
- Baker's Yeast (*Saccharomyces cerevisiae*) is used to make bread, beer and wine, during which process sugars such as glucose or sucrose are fermented to make alcohol and · carbon dioxide. In the case of bread-making, the alcohol evaporates and the carbon dioxide serves to make the dough rise.
- Enzymes of *Penicillium camemberti* play a role in the manufacture of the cheeses Camembert and Brie, while those of *Penicillium roqueforti* do the same for Gorgonzola, Roquefort and Stilton.
- In Asia *Aspergillus oryzae* is added to a pulp of soaked soya beans to make soy sauce.
- Finally, some members of the Ascomycota are eaten with relish; morels (*Morchella*) and truffles (*Tuber*) are some of the most sought-after fungus delicacies.

# Index

❑❑❑